Ecology and Religion in History

EDITED BY

David and
Eileen Spring

HARPER TORCHBOOKS
Harper & Row, Publishers
New York, Hagerstown, San Francisco, London

ECOLOGY AND RELIGION IN HISTORY

For information address Harper & Row, Publishers, Inc., 10 East 53d Street, New York, N.Y. 10022. Published simultaneously in Canada by Fitzhenry & Whiteside Limited, Toronto.

First HARPER TORCHBOOK edition published 1974
LIBRARY OF CONGRESS CATALOG CARD NUMBER: 74–6580
STANDARD BOOK NUMBER: 06–131829–9 (PAPERBACK)
78 79 80 12 11 10 9 8 7 6 5 4 3

20¢

Ecology and Religion in History

the text of this book is printed on 100% recycled paper

BASIC CONDITIONS OF LIFE

Robert and Elborg Forster, eds.	European Diet from Pre-Industrial to Modern Times
Joseph and Barrie Klaits, eds.	Animals and Man in Historical Perspective
Michael R. Marrus, ed.	The Emergence of Leisure
Orest and Patricia Ranum, eds.	Popular Attitudes toward Birth Control in Pre-Industrial France and England
Edward Shorter, ed.	Work and Community in the West
David and Eileen Spring, eds.	Ecology and Religion in History

Contents

Acknowledgments

The editors wish to thank James Barr, John Macquarrie, Lewis Moncrief, Yi-Fu Tuan, Arnold Toynbee, and Lynn White for permission to reprint their articles.

The following journals have also kindly given their permission for the reprinting of these articles: *Bulletin of the John Rylands Library, The Canadian Geographer, The Expository Times, The International Journal of Environmental Studies,* and *Science.*

The editors are also grateful to René Dubos as author and Charles Scribner's Sons as publisher for permission to reprint a chapter of *A God Within.*

Introduction

We live in a world that is increasingly marked by environmental degradation. We suffer from pollution, noise, and crowding. We witness the destruction of innumerable pleasant landscapes and are aware of the threatened extinction of many beautiful and interesting forms of life. Ecological problems have become, in the words of this series, a basic condition of our life.

What are the historical roots of these problems, problems that taken together are often justly spoken of as our ecological crisis? To what degree are the roots of our problems to be found in religion? Over the past generation a number of those who have reflected upon man's condition have pointed to a religious failure—to a failure in man to relate himself morally to the natural world. Thinkers from different disciplines and of different outlooks have pointed to this failure.

Albert Schweitzer, for example, remarked in a well-known sentence, "The great fault of all ethics hitherto has been that they believed themselves to have to deal only with the relations of man to man."[1] Aldo Leopold, a biologist who is also an essayist of charm, lamented in his *Sand County Almanac* the lack of what he called a "land ethic." Land, he protests, like Odysseus' slave girls, is still property. Our relations to it are still "strictly economic, entailing privileges but not obligations."[2]

1. Albert Schweitzer, *Out of My Life and Thought* (New York, 1933), p. 188.
2. Aldo Leopold, *A Sand County Almanac* (New York, 1966), pp. 214–241.

This theme is carried further by Joseph Wood Krutch, a literary critic turned naturalist, in a moving article, "Conservation Is Not Enough."[3]

Representing what we may be pleased to think is a more practical point of view are the reflections of Carl Sauer, a noted geographer. Surveying man's work upon the face of the earth he wonders if "our newly found powers to transform the world . . . are proper and wise beyond the tenure of those now living." Apparently they are not, for Sauer concludes that man needs a revised ethic and aesthetic.[4] Somewhat similar are the reflections of the anthropologist Claude Lévi-Strauss. Noting that maggots in a sack of flour can become so numerous that their activity poisons the flour and they thereby bring on their own extinction, Lévi-Strauss wonders whether man may not similarly annihilate himself through poisoning the biosphere. He concludes that man will save himself only by profound spiritual change.[5]

These are important—even revolutionary—insights. Nevertheless they are substantially indictments and warnings. They do not explain why we take the attitude to nature that we do. Recently, however, an explanation has been offered. In a provocative article Lynn White has put forward the thesis that the root cause of our ecological problems is to be found in the Judeo-Christian ethic.

This article has aroused widespread discussion. It has echoed through academic publications. It has come to the ears of the world at large and is to be found discussed in the pages of such

3. This article was originally published in the *American Scholar,* 23, no. 3 (Summer 1954), 295–305. It has been reprinted in two books by Joseph Wood Krutch, *The Voice of the Desert* (New York, 1955) and *The World of Animals* (New York, 1961).
4. Carl O. Sauer, "The Agency of Man on Earth," in *Man's Role in Changing the Face of the Earth,* ed. William L. Thomas, Jr. (Chicago, 1956), pp. 49–69.
5. Claude Lévi-Strauss, interview in the *New York Times,* 31 December 1969.

diverse journals as the *New York Times* and the *Oracle,* the latter a one-time hippie newspaper. It has stirred up a movement of reform—the Faith/Man/Nature group—within the Christian community. It has emboldened an influential animal welfare society to analyze with unwonted candor the causes of cruelty to animals. It is an article that prompts us to look at the world with new-seeing eyes and to take stock of inherited preconceptions that have long gone unexamined.

To discuss religion and ecology in history is largely to discuss the Lynn White article. The readings in this book therefore consist of this article together with some of the more important commentaries it has elicited. The commentaries represent different disciplines. Their authors are an ecologist, a geographer, a social scientist, and two theologians. Included also is a paper by a great historian who, apparently independently, has come to conclusions similar to White's.

The readings do not build upon one another in logical sequence. They are, rather, parallel reflections; each starts afresh and makes its points in isolation. To give coherence to the whole, it may be useful in this introduction to place the readings in the wider discussion to which they belong, both pointing up the issues involved in the discussion and indicating what each reading particularly contributes to it.

White's thesis may be very briefly summarized. White believes that by emphasizing the dominion of man over nature Christianity has sanctioned an exploitative ethic. He further believes that Christianity has thereby fostered science and technology. Since these are forces that now pose—even in their peaceful use—manifold threats to the environment and possibly even to the life of our planet, it follows that Christianity "bears a huge burden of guilt" for our ecologic crisis. This thesis, it may be noted, is the work of a man well fitted to formulate it. Lynn

White is a Christian thinker, the author of articles reflecting upon the religious meaning of history. He is also a distinguished historian who specializes in the technology of the Middle Ages.

The discussion that has attended this thesis has centered upon three ideas—upon the two leading ideas explicit in the thesis and upon another that is assumed by it.

First, there is the idea that Christianity has taught an ethic unsympathetic to the natural world. There undeniably are biblical injunctions that easily may be so interpreted. And undeniably these injunctions are fundamental. They are to be found in the Creation story and are intended to set out the basic relations between man and nature. Thus, in Genesis 1:28, God instructs Adam:

> *Be fruitful, and multiply, and replenish the earth, and subdue it: and have dominion over the fish of the sea, and over the fowl of the air, and over every living thing that moveth upon the earth.*

And so in Genesis 9:2, God repeats for Noah after the flood:

> *And the fear of you and the dread of you shall be upon every beast of the earth, and upon every fowl of the air, upon all that moveth upon the earth, and upon all the fishes of the sea; into your hand are they delivered.*

White has told how he was first led to formulate his thesis by watching Buddhists in Ceylon build a road.[6] Noting cones of earth left undisturbed upon the intended roadbed, he discovered that these were the nests of snakes. The Buddhists would not destroy the cones until the snakes departed of their own accord

6. Lynn White, "Continuing the Conversation" in *Western Man and Environmental Ethics,* ed. Ian Barbour (Reading, Mass., 1973), p. 55.

from the scene of activity. Among other things, White could not help reflecting that had the road builders been Christian, the snakes would have suffered a different fate.

This story provokes a smile. We find the Buddhists quaintly inefficient. At the same time we are made uneasy. Buddhism sets skeletons to rattling in Christian closets. We are reminded what outlandish and unnecessary cruelties have been—and are—acceptable in the Christian world. One need only reflect upon the fur trade. Christian men trekked over a primeval continent dealing an unconscionably cruel death to millions of animals for no necessary reason—beaver skins going to satisfy nothing but the vanity of the rich. This activity went unremarked by the Church. So too did the elaborate development of sports hunting—hunting indulged in either for frivolous reasons or for no reason but the desire to kill. Gavin Maxwell, who has written so charmingly of otters, has told how two of his cubs playing on the shore were shot by a passing clergyman. The clergyman reminded the press that "The Lord gave man control over the beasts of the field. . . ."[7]

The assent given to this sort of activity indicates meager Christian regard for animal life, and implies even less for plants, or rocks, or soil. It may be concluded—and probably is so obvious that it needed no illustration—that Christians have often interpreted Genesis arrogantly. They have believed it gives man a dominion over nature that is absolute. Through Christianity Western man has come to assume that nature exists for no other reason than to minister to man. The biologist Marston Bates ruefully testifies to the continuing strength of this attitude. He finds that people coming across some natural object unfamil-

7. C. F. D. Moule, *Man and Nature in the New Testament* (Philadelphia, 1967), p. 1.

iar to them do not ask, "What is its role in the scheme of things?" or, "What part does it play in nature?"—questions that would indicate minds influenced by Galileo and Darwin to acknowledge the independent existence of the universe. Rather they perplex a biologist how even to begin to reply by asking with appalling unselfconciousness, "What good is it?"[8]

It is often pointed out in discussions of White's thesis that this arrogant attitude is not the only one to be found in Christianity. Christianity is a complex religion capable of different interpretations. The injunctions of Genesis can be more humbly interpreted. They may mean that man is to exercise his dominion responsibly as a steward of God, for Adam was put into the Garden of Eden "to dress and to keep it." More conspicuously, Christianity has produced a saint who greatly loved nature.

The constancy with which the Church refers to St. Francis whenever its attitude to nature is questioned once led a humanitarian reformer to suspect "that its choice must be but a limited one."[9] He voiced a suspicion that White makes it a point to affirm. White himself suggests reviving the ideas of St. Francis, but he does not believe that St. Francis was typical of the Church. Indeed he emphasizes that St. Francis verged on heresy. Nor does he believe that the doctrine of stewardship has been a dominant force in Christianity.[10] For a historian, Christianity is what ordinary Christians have usually thought it to be, and ordinary Christians have not often felt themselves restrained by their religion from doing whatever they pleased with nature. The question thus at issue here is not whether a kindly and humble attitude to nature has existed in Christianity, but

8. Marston Bates, *The Forest and the Sea* (New York, 1960), p. 4.
9. H. S. Salt, *Seventy Years among Savages* (New York, 1921), p. 213.
10. Lynn White, Jr., letter in *Science,* 156 (12 May 1967), 737.

whether it has been the dominant attitude.

White intended his article as a plea that the arrogant attitude toward nature be abandoned. This attitude has encouraged man to ravage the earth and he is likely to continue to do so until he rejects it. As a result of the article there has been candid rethinking of Christian doctrine. A spate of books indicates that many Christians have been set to searching their faith for latent ideas more appropriate to the needs of today.[11] Some look to Franciscanism, others to ideas of stewardship. In a reading in this book, John Macquarrie reexamines theism itself and finds latent in Christianity an organic conception of God that would tend to promote a better attitude to the natural world. He also makes illuminating suggestions as to how Christianity came to acquire its present emphasis.

The second idea contained in White's thesis concerns the relation of Christianity to science and technology. White does more than charge that Christianity has taught an ethic unsympathetic to the natural world. He believes that the Christian ethic has worked itself out in a particularly momentous way in Western history. He believes that it has made possible and has fostered the development of science and technology. These are, for White, the "realization of the Christian dogma of man's transcendence of and rightful mastery over nature."

A comparison of the pre-Christian and the Christian outlooks elucidates the connection between science and Christianity. The pantheistic religions of Greece and Rome held that all natural phenomena were infused with divinity; springs and hills, fields and woods were the abode of gods or guardian spirits. Pantheis-

11. See for example, Ian Barbour, ed., *Earth Might Be Fair* (Englewood Cliffs, N.J., 1972); John Black, *Dominion of Man* (Edinburgh, 1970); Frederick Elder, *Crisis in Eden* (Nashville, Tenn., 1970); and Michael Hamilton, ed., *This Little Planet* (New York, 1970).

tic man therefore approached nature with respect, and was inhibited in his exploitation of it. Christianity, on the other hand, because of its anthropocentric Creation story approaches nature in a matter-of-fact way, in a "mood of indifference to the feelings of natural objects." Nature has become an object to be used. Clearly the pantheistic attitude conflicts with the inquiring, manipulative attitude of science, and the Christian accords with it. Thus, Christianity may be said to have introduced to the world the attitude that is the prerequisite of science and technology.

Christianity not only made science possible but also gave it active encouragement. While the Christian did not believe that God is in nature he did believe that nature is God's creation. It followed that man could discern the mind of God by observing and understanding nature's ways. There developed as a result an extensive literature of natural theology that is sometimes hard to distinguish from science.

No one can deny that there is truth in the idea that Christianity has encouraged the development of science and technology. Indeed, a number of theologians, particularly Harvey Cox in *The Secular City,* have earlier asserted it.[12] They did so when technology went unquestioned as a good. What White has done is to document the idea from his great knowledge of medieval technology, and to reassert it while burdened with the awareness that technology has come to threaten man's future. In a reading in this book Arnold Toynbee supports and elaborates the idea. Toynbee, who was educated both as a Christian scholar and as a classical scholar, feels in his bones the difference in outlook to nature between the Judeo-Christian world and the classical world. He points out particularly that monotheism tends logi-

12. Harvey Cox, *The Secular City* (New York, 1965).

cally toward the exploitation of nature; by concentrating divinity solely in one transcendent God, monotheism effectively removes divinity from nature and thereby unleashes man's greed.

While Christianity has thus had an influence upon the development of science and technology, it may nevertheless be doubted whether that influence has been vital or preponderating. Questions subversive of the idea, or at least needing answer before it is accepted, suggest themselves. How is it that ordinarily we are not only unaware of the connection between faith and science but are likely to sense a conflict between the two? Why did the Eastern Orthodox branch of Christianity not develop a science? And why did the ancient Jews, who shared with Christians both a monotheistic God and the same Creation story, not do so either?

Two authors in this book deny the close relationship of Christianity and science. Lewis Moncrief has Christianity a cause of science and technology but only tenuously. Moreover, he notes that science and technology have been abetted by largely secular forces such as capitalism and democracy. In such a view the roots of our ecological troubles are better sought near at hand in these forces than further afield in religion. James Barr also believes Christianity to be but remotely connected to science. He comes to the belief from a detailed examination not of secular forces but of Old Testament attitudes.

This is a debate that is not likely to be soon ended. Weighing the effect of religious ideas upon great secular developments is notoriously difficult. Early in this century Max Weber put forward the thesis that the Protestant ethic was largely responsible for the growth of capitalism. He thereby touched off what White himself has called "the academic Thirty Years War."[13] For over

13. Lynn White, Jr., "The Iconography of *Temperantia* and the Virtuousness

a generation historians and theologians argued over Weber's thesis, and occasionally they still do. It may well be that another such debate is in the making.

Finally, as we mentioned earlier, there is an idea assumed in White's thesis. As tends to be true of assumed ideas, it is one that concerns fundamentals. White assumes that what men think about nature much affects what they do about nature; he assumes that religion or philosophy *has* ecological consequences. That ideas matter very much in human affairs is, of course, a widespread assumption. Not only do theologians and historians proceed upon it in their professional work, but so too do ordinary people in everyday life. Thus White's assumption is concurred in even by many who otherwise criticize his thesis. In the realm of ecology, however, how valid is this assumption? Is it true that what men have thought about nature has much affected what they have done to nature? What indeed have ecologists and natural scientists generally to say of White's thesis?

Ecologists and natural scientists are not of a single mind about it. On the one hand, many of them refer to it with evident approval, and many themselves suggest the necessity for spiritual reformation if man is to solve his ecological problems. On the other hand, there has been one recurrent vein of criticism among ecologists and natural scientists that would go to modify, or to add to, the thesis.

Natural scientists often point out that man has been altering his environment ever since he developed settled agriculture. He has cut and burned forests to build houses and to create fields;

---

of Technology," in *Action and Conviction in Early Modern Europe: Essays in Memory of E. H. Harbison*, ed. T. K. Rabb and J. E. Seigel (Princeton, N.J., 1969), p. 197.

he has drained marshes; he has dug in the earth for minerals, clay, and stone. Everywhere and for a long time man has been rearranging the landscape to suit himself. It has recently been suggested that man was an ecological force even before he developed settled agriculture. Primitive man, using fire as a hunting tool, may have helped drive the great Pleistocene mammals to extinction. Man has not always been destructive of nature, but in many places and in many ages he has been. He has caused deforestation and soil erosion from China to the Middle East, from Central America to sub-Saharan Africa. In other words, man has been destructive of nature no matter what his religion and even when he has lacked sophisticated technology. In an essay in this book, Yi-Fu Tuan wryly points to many discrepancies that can be found between what men have said about nature and what men have done to nature.

Natural scientists thus often tend to think that White's view has not been extensive enough. When they take an extended view of man's actions upon the earth they find religious ideas of less importance than biological facts such as the fragility of particular environments, the number of men trying to live in each, and the characteristics of man as a species. They are likely to stress—when they don't despair—the importance for man of learning to think ecologically. This is the burden of the selection in this book by René Dubos. Man, says Dubos, has committed his environmental follies not because he has been influenced by the Bible, but largely because he has been ecologically ignorant. What is needed to overcome our ecological problems is therefore less a spiritual reformation than an increase in knowledge. If man studies both his past successes and his past failures he will learn how to read nature better. He will accordingly better manage her, or better adjust himself to her.

What the natural scientists show is, in a sense, indisputable.

Our current technological attack on nature is the latest of many that man, professing a great variety of religions, has made upon the earth. This view gives valuable insights into the causes of our ecological troubles. It makes us consider in a biological way what is the place of man in nature and what are the limits of the biosphere. In particular it brings to our attention what seems a fundamental problem of human behavior—the tendency of man to breed beyond the limits of his environment. A noted biologist, V. C. Wynne-Edwards, has recently made clear that this behavior is abnormal among animals.[14] In a work that has been compared to Darwin's in importance, Wynne-Edwards has demonstrated that animals normally have breeding habits that prevent them from destroying their environment. He is not referring to predation. He means that animals have self-regulatory mechanisms by which the number of young born is limited to the carrying capacity of the environment. Did man once have similar habits? If so, how has he lost them? Clearly, biologists and ethologists have much to say about the causes of our ecological crisis.

To summarize, the view of many natural scientists may be said to stress the constancy with which man has scarred his environment. It tends to see our technological attack on nature as the continuation of a common or natural trend, different only in magnitude from the attacks of the past. In this view, religious ideas may play a role in ecological affairs, but that role is secondary.

14. V. C. Wynne-Edwards, *Animal Dispersion in Relation to Social Behavior* (New York, 1962). For a succinct nontechnical summary of this work, see V. C. Wynne-Edwards, "Self-Regulating Systems in Populations of Animals," *Science,* 147 (26 March 1965), 1543–1548. This article has been reprinted in Paul Shepard and Daniel McKinley, eds., *The Subversive Science* (Boston, 1969).

While this view is undoubtedly valuable, it may in turn have limitations as an explanation of our current problems. In emphasizing the constant factor in man's ecological history it tends to obscure differences. It tends in particular to obscure the violence of the technological attack on nature. In so doing, it is possible that it underestimates the significance of the Christian religion.

This view of man's ecological problems tends to compare soil erosion effected by peasants over thousands of years with the planet-wide degradation effected by modern man in a few generations. It tends to compare things that it may be as appropriate to contrast as to compare. Western science, for example, has given an explosive force to man's population growth. Industrial man consumes natural resources at a rate at least fifty times that of his agricultural ancestors. Twenty-five years—a moment of time—is all it has taken for a biocide released by industrial man to appear in the bodies of men everywhere and even in the bodies of animals living in the Antarctic. In its vast scale and frenzied tempo the technological attack on nature may be said to be unprecedented. This is the starting point of White's thesis. In his words, "the impact of our race upon the environment has so increased in force that it has changed its essence."

The issue here between White and his critics is thus the meaning of this change of scale. Significantly perhaps, the meaning of this change of scale is the issue upon which a related ecological debate, that on the limits to economic growth, has also come to turn. Ever since the Club of Rome published its computer-based study predicting ecological collapse within a century if present trends continue, many economists have countered by pointing out that man's history demonstrates that he has been repeatedly, continously successful in overcoming shortages and environmental problems in the past. A group of scientists finds the thinking of the economists complacent. In support of the Club of Rome they say: "The basic flaw in [the economists'] approach, and the reason that all analogies from ancient Greece or Egypt are totally irrelevant, is [their] failure to understand the significance of the relative orders of magnitude. . . . This question of scale is absolutely fundamental. . . ."[15]

There is thus a sense in which the technological attack upon nature is not a continuation of the past but marks a break with it; a sense in which the technological attack is something new under the sun. It is therefore possible to take the view that this attack is not, for the most part, to be explained as earlier attacks are to be explained. It is reasonable to seek the cause of this attack in something peculiar to Western history. White finds the cause to be in Christianity, for Christianity fundamentally altered man's way of looking at nature. For the Christian, man was no longer a part of nature; man was the center of Creation, and he had a positive injunction to subdue nature. Christianity thus provided "a set of presuppositions remarkably favorable to technological thrust."[16] In short, one may note the facts that ecology points out and yet hold that religious ideas are a prime cause of our ecological crisis.

Such are the issues that White's thesis raises. They are issues that disturb fundamental beliefs and habitual actions. Yet they are ones vital for modern man to reflect upon.

15. Lowell S. Brown et al., "Are There Real Limits to Growth?—A Reply to Beckerman," *Oxford Economic Papers,* 25 (1973), 456.
16. White, "Continuing the Conversation," p. 58.

The Historical Roots of Our Ecologic Crisis

LYNN WHITE, JR.

A conversation with Aldous Huxley not infrequently put one at the receiving end of an unforgettable monologue. About a year before his lamented death he was discoursing on a favorite topic: Man's unnatural treatment of nature and its sad results. To illustrate his point he told how, during the previous summer, he had returned to a little valley in England where he had spent many happy months as a child. Once it had been composed of delightful grassy glades; now it was becoming overgrown with unsightly brush because the rabbits that formerly kept such growth under control had largely succumbed to a disease, myxomatosis, that was deliberately introduced by the local farmers to reduce the rabbits' destruction of crops. Being something of a Philistine, I could be silent no longer, even in the interests of great rhetoric. I interrupted to point out that the rabbit itself had been brought as a domestic animal to England in 1176,

SOURCE: *Science,* 155 (10 March 1967), 1203–1207. Copyright 1967 by the American Association for the Advancement of Science. Reprinted by permission of *Science* and the author. This article was delivered at a meeting of the American Association for the Advancement of Science in Washington, D.C., 26 December 1966.

presumably to improve the protein diet of the peasantry.

All forms of life modify their contexts. The most spectacular and benign instance is doubtless the coral polyp. By serving its own ends, it has created a vast undersea world favorable to thousands of other kinds of animals and plants. Ever since man became a numerous species he has affected his environment notably. The hypothesis that his fire-drive method of hunting created the world's great grasslands and helped to exterminate the monster mammals of the Pleistocene from much of the globe is plausible, if not proved. For 6 millennia at least, the banks of the lower Nile have been a human artifact rather than the swampy African jungle which nature, apart from man, would have made it. The Aswan Dam, flooding 5000 square miles, is only the latest stage in a long process. In many regions terracing or irrigation, overgrazing, the cutting of forests by Romans to build ships to fight Carthaginians or by Crusaders to solve the logistics problems of their expeditions, have profoundly changed some ecologies. Observation that the French landscape falls into two basic types, the open fields of the north and the *bocage* of the south and west, inspired Marc Bloch to undertake his classic study of medieval agricultural methods. Quite unintentionally, changes in human ways often affect nonhuman nature. It has been noted, for example, that the advent of the automobile eliminated huge flocks of sparrows that once fed on the horse manure littering every street.

The history of ecologic change is still so rudimentary that we know little about what really happened, or what the results were. The extinction of the European aurochs as late as 1627 would seem to have been a simple case of overenthusiastic hunting. On more intricate matters it often is impossible to find solid information. For a thousand years or more the Frisians and Hollanders have been pushing back the North Sea, and the process is culminating in our own time in the reclamation of the Zuider Zee. What, if any, species of animals, birds, fish, shore life, or plants have died out in the process? In their epic combat with Neptune have the Netherlanders overlooked ecological values in such a way that the quality of human life in the Netherlands has suffered? I cannot discover that the questions have ever been asked, much less answered.

People, then, have often been a dynamic element in their own environment, but in the present state of historical scholarship we usually do not know exactly when, where, or with what effects man-induced changes came. As we enter the last third of the 20th century, however, concern for the problem of ecologic backlash is mounting feverishly. Natural science, conceived as the effort to understand the nature of things, had flourished in several eras and among several peoples. Similarly there had been an age-old accumulation of technological skills, sometimes growing rapidly, sometimes slowly. But it was not until about four generations ago that Western Europe and North America arranged a marriage between science and technology, a union of the theoretical and the empirical approaches to our natural environment. The emergence in widespread practice of the Baconian creed that scientific knowledge means technological power over nature can scarcely be dated before about 1850, save in the chemical industries, where it is anticipated in the 18th century. Its acceptance as a normal pattern of action may mark the greatest event in human history since the invention of agriculture, and perhaps in nonhuman terrestrial history as well.

Almost at once the new situation forced the crystallization of the novel concept of ecology; indeed, the word *ecology* first appeared in the English language in 1873. Today, less than a century later, the impact of our race upon the environment has so increased in force that it has changed in essence. When the first cannons were fired, in the early 14th century, they affected ecology by sending workers scrambling to the forests and mountains for more potash, sulfur, iron ore, and charcoal, with some resulting erosion and deforestation. Hydrogen bombs are of a different order: a war fought with them might alter the genetics of all life on this planet. By 1285 London had a smog problem arising from the burning of soft coal, but our present combustion of fossil fuels threatens to change the chemistry of the globe's atmosphere as a whole, with consequences which we are only beginning to guess. With the population explosion, the carcinoma of planless urbanism, the now geological deposits of sewage and garbage, surely no creature other than man has ever managed to foul its nest in such short order.

There are many calls to action, but specific proposals, however worthy as individual items, seem too partial, palliative, negative: ban the bomb, tear down the billboards, give the Hindus contraceptives and tell them to eat their sacred cows. The simplest solution to any suspect change is, of course, to stop it, or, better yet, to revert to a romanticized past: make those ugly gasoline stations look like Anne Hathaway's cottage or (in the Far West) like ghost-town saloons. The "wilderness area" mentality invariably advocates deep-freezing an ecology, whether San Gimignano or the High Sierra, as it was before the first Kleenex was dropped. But neither atavism nor prettification will cope with the ecologic crisis of our time.

What shall we do? No one yet knows. Unless we think about fundamentals, our specific measures may produce new backlashes more serious than those they are designed to remedy.

As a beginning we should try to clarify our thinking by looking, in some historical depth, at the presuppositions that underlie modern technology and science. Science was traditionally aristocratic, speculative, intellectual in intent; technology was lower-class, empirical, action-oriented. The quite sudden fusion of these two, towards the middle of the 19th century, is surely related to the slightly prior and contemporary democratic revolutions which, by reducing social barriers, tended to assert a functional unity of brain and hand. Our ecologic crisis is the product of an emerging, entirely novel, democratic culture. The issue is whether a democratized world can survive its own implications. Presumably we cannot unless we rethink our axioms.

THE WESTERN TRADITIONS OF TECHNOLOGY AND SCIENCE

One thing is so certain that it seems stupid to verbalize it: both modern technology and modern science are distinctively *Occidental.* Our technology has absorbed elements from all over the world, notably from China; yet everywhere today, whether in Japan or in Nigeria, successful technology is Western. Our science is the heir to all the sciences of the past, especially perhaps to the work of the great Islamic scientists of the Middle Ages, who so often outdid the ancient Greeks in skill and perspicacity: al-Rāzī in medicine, for example; or ibn-al-Haytham in optics; or Omar Khayyám in mathematics. Indeed, not a few works of such geniuses seem to have vanished in the original Arabic and to survive only in medieval Latin translations that helped to lay the foundations for later Western developments. Today, around the globe, all significant science is Western in style and method, whatever the pigmentation or language of the scientists.

A second pair of facts is less well recognized because they result from quite recent historical scholarship. The leadership of the West, both in technology and in science, is far older than the so-called Scientific Revolution of the 17th century or the so-called Industrial Revolution of the 18th century. These terms are in fact outmoded and obscure the true nature of what they try to describe—significant stages in two long and separate developments. By A.D. 1000 at the latest—and perhaps, feebly, as much as 200 years earlier—the West began to apply water power to industrial processes other than milling grain. This was followed in the late 12th century by the harnessing of wind power. From simple beginnings, but with remarkable consistency of style, the West rapidly expanded its skills in the development of power machinery, labor-saving devices, and automation. Those who doubt should contemplate that most monumental achievement in the history of automation: the weight-driven mechanical clock, which appeared in two forms in the early 14th century. Not in craftsmanship but in basic technological capacity, the Latin West of the later Middle Ages far outstripped its elaborate, sophisticated, and esthetically magnificent sister cultures, Byzantium and Islam. In 1444 a great Greek ecclesiastic, Bessarion, who had gone to Italy, wrote a letter to a prince in Greece. He is amazed by the superiority of Western ships, arms, textiles, glass. But above all he is astonished by the spectacle of waterwheels sawing timbers and pumping the bellows of blast furnaces. Clearly, he had seen nothing of the sort in the Near East.

By the end of the 15th century the technological superiority of Europe was such that its small, mutually hostile nations could spill out over all the rest of the world, conquering, looting, and colonizing. The symbol of this technological superiority is the fact that Portugal, one of the weakest states of the Occident, was able to become, and to remain for a century, mistress of the East Indies. And we must remember that the technology of Vasco da

Gama and Albuquerque was built by pure empiricism, drawing remarkably little support or inspiration from science.

In the present-day vernacular understanding, modern science is supposed to have begun in 1543, when both Copernicus and Vesalius published their great works. It is no derogation of their accomplishments, however, to point out that such structures as the *Fabrica* and the *De revolutionibus* do not appear overnight. The distinctive Western tradition of science, in fact, began in the late 11th century with a massive movement of translation of Arabic and Greek scientific works into Latin. A few notable books—Theophrastus, for example—escaped the West's avid new appetite for science, but within less than 200 years effectively the entire corpus of Greek and Muslim science was available in Latin, and was being eagerly read and criticized in the new European universities. Out of criticism arose new observation, speculation, and increasing distrust of ancient authorities. By the late 13th century Europe had seized global scientific leadership from the faltering hands of Islam. It would be as absurd to deny the profound originality of Newton, Galileo, or Copernicus as to deny that of the 14th century scholastic scientists like Buridan or Oresme on whose work they built. Before the 11th century, science scarcely existed in the Latin West, even in Roman times. From the 11th century onward, the scientific sector of Occidental culture has increased in a steady crescendo.

Since both our technological and our scientific movements got their start, acquired their character, and achieved world dominance in the Middle Ages, it would seem that we cannot understand their nature or their present impact upon ecology without examining fundamental medieval assumptions and developments.

MEDIEVAL VIEW OF MAN AND NATURE

Until recently, agriculture has been the chief occupation even in "advanced" societies; hence, any change in methods of tillage has much importance. Early plows, drawn by two oxen, did not normally turn the sod but merely scratched it. Thus, cross-plowing was needed and fields tended to be squarish. In the fairly light soils and semiarid climates of the Near East and Mediterranean, this worked well. But such a plow was inappropriate to the wet climate and often sticky soils of northern Europe. By the latter part of the 7th century after Christ, however, following obscure beginnings, certain northern peasants were using an entirely new kind of plow, equipped with a vertical knife to cut the line of the furrow, a horizontal share to slice under the sod, and a moldboard to turn it over. The friction of this plow with the soil was so great that it normally required not two but eight oxen. It attacked the land with such violence that cross-plowing was not needed, and fields tended to be shaped in long strips.

In the days of the scratch-plow, fields were distributed generally in units capable of supporting a single family. Subsistence farming was the presupposition. But no peasant owned eight oxen: to use the new and more efficient plow, peasants pooled their oxen to form large plow-teams, originally receiving (it would appear) plowed strips in proportion to their contribution. Thus, distribution of land was based no longer on the needs of a family but, rather, on the capacity of a power machine to till the earth. Man's relation to the soil was profoundly changed. Formerly man had been part of nature; now he was the exploiter of nature. Nowhere else in the world did farmers develop any analogous agricultural implement. Is it coincidence that modern technology, with its ruthlessness toward nature, has so largely been produced by descendants of these peasants of northern Europe?

This same exploitive attitude appears slightly before A.D. 830 in Western illustrated calendars. In older calendars the months were shown as passive personifications. The new Frankish calendars, which set the style for the Middle Ages, are very different: they show men coercing the world around them—plowing, harvesting, chopping trees, butchering pigs. Man and nature are two things, and man is master.

These novelties seem to be in harmony with larger intellectual patterns. What people do about their ecology depends on what they think about themselves in relation to things around them. Human ecology is deeply conditioned by beliefs about our nature and destiny—that is, by religion. To Western eyes this is very evident in, say, India or Ceylon. It is equally true of ourselves and of our medieval ancestors.

The victory of Christianity over paganism was the greatest psychic revolution in the history of our culture. It has become fashionable today to say that, for better or worse, we live in "the post-Christian age." Certainly the forms of our thinking and language have largely ceased to be Christian, but to my eye the substance often remains amazingly akin to that of the past. Our daily habits of action, for example, are dominated by an implicit faith in perpetual progress which was unknown either to Greco-Roman antiquity or to the Orient. It is rooted in, and is indefensible apart from, Judeo-Christian teleology. The fact that Communists share it merely helps to show what can be demonstrated on many other grounds: that Marxism, like Islam, is a Judeo-Christian heresy. We continue today to live, as we have lived for about 1700 years, very largely in a context of Christian axioms.

What did Christianity tell people about their relations with the environment?

While many of the world's mythologies provide stories of creation, Greco-Roman mythology was singularly incoherent in this respect. Like Aristotle, the intellectuals of the ancient West denied that the visible world had had a beginning. Indeed, the idea of a beginning was impossible in the framework of their cyclical notion of time. In sharp contrast, Christianity inherited from Judaism not only a concept of time as nonrepetitive and linear but also a striking story of creation. By gradual stages a loving and all-powerful God had created light and darkness, the heavenly bodies, the earth and all its plants, animals, birds, and fishes. Finally, God had created Adam and, as an afterthought, Eve to keep man from being lonely. Man named all the animals, thus establishing his dominance over them. God planned all of this explicitly for man's benefit and rule: no item in the physical creation had any purpose save to serve man's purposes. And, although man's body is made of clay, he is not simply part of nature: he is made in God's image.

Especially in its Western form, Christianity is the most anthropocentric religion the world has seen. As early as the 2nd century both Tertullian and Saint Irenaeus of Lyons were insisting that when God shaped Adam he was foreshadowing the image of the incarnate Christ, the Second Adam. Man shares, in great measure, God's transcendence of nature. Christianity, in absolute contrast to ancient paganism and Asia's religions (except, perhaps, Zoroastrianism), not only established a dualism of man and nature but also insisted that it is God's will that man exploit nature for his proper ends.

At the level of the common people this worked out in an interesting way. In Antiquity every tree, every spring, every stream, every hill had its own *genius loci,* its guardian spirit. These spirits were accessible to men, but were very unlike men; centaurs, fauns, and mermaids show their ambivalence. Before one cut a tree, mined a mountain, or dammed a brook, it was important to placate the spirit in charge of that particular situation, and to keep it placated. By destroying pagan animism, Christianity made it possible to exploit nature in a mood of indifference to the feelings of natural objects.

It is often said that for animism the Church substituted the cult of saints. True; but the cult of saints is functionally quite different from animism. The saint is not *in* natural objects; he may have special shrines, but his citizenship is in heaven. Moreover, a saint is entirely a man; he can be approached in human terms. In addition to saints, Christianity of course also had angels and demons inherited from Judaism and perhaps, at one remove, from Zoroastrianism. But these were all as mobile as the saints themselves. The spirits *in* natural objects, which formerly had protected nature from man, evaporated. Man's effective monopoly on spirit in this world was confirmed, and the old inhibitions to the exploitation of nature crumbled.

When one speaks in such sweeping terms, a note of caution is in order. Christianity is a complex faith, and its consequences differ in differing contexts. What I have said may well apply to the medieval West, where in fact technology made spectacular advances. But the Greek East, a highly civilized realm of equal Christian devotion, seems to have produced no marked technological innovation after the late 7th century, when Greek fire was invented. The key to the contrast may perhaps be found in a difference in the tonality of piety and thought which students of comparative theology find between the Greek and the Latin Churches. The Greeks believed that sin was intellectual blindness, and that salvation was found in illumination, orthodoxy—

that is, clear thinking. The Latins, on the other hand, felt that sin was moral evil, and that salvation was to be found in right conduct. Eastern theology has been intellectualist. Western theology has been voluntarist. The Greek saint contemplates; the Western saint acts. The implications of Christianity for the conquest of nature would emerge more easily in the Western atmosphere.

The Christian dogma of creation, which is found in the first clause of all the Creeds, has another meaning for our comprehension of today's ecologic crisis. By revelation, God had given man the Bible, the Book of Scripture. But since God had made nature, nature also must reveal the divine mentality. The religious study of nature for the better understanding of God was known as natural theology. In the early Church, and always in the Greek East, nature was conceived primarily as a symbolic system through which God speaks to men: the ant is a sermon to sluggards; rising flames are the symbol of the soul's aspiration. This view of nature was essentially artistic rather than scientific. While Byzantium preserved and copied great numbers of ancient Greek scientific texts, science as we conceive it could scarcely flourish in such an ambience.

However, in the Latin West by the early 13th century natural theology was following a very different bent. It was ceasing to be the decoding of the physical symbols of God's communication with man and was becoming the effort to understand God's mind by discovering how his creation operates. The rainbow was no longer simply a symbol of hope first sent to Noah after the Deluge: Robert Grosseteste, Friar Roger Bacon, and Theodoric of Freiberg produced startlingly sophisticated work on the optics of the rainbow, but they did it as a venture in religious understanding. From the 13th century onward, up to and including Leibnitz and Newton, every major scientist, in effect, explained his motivations in religious terms. Indeed, if Galileo had not been so expert an amateur theologian he would have got into far less trouble: the professionals resented his intrusion. And Newton seems to have regarded himself more as a theologian than as a scientist. It was not until the late 18th century that the hypothesis of God became unnecessary to many scientists.

It is often hard for the historian to judge, when men explain why they are doing what they want to do, whether they are offering real reasons or merely culturally acceptable reasons. The consistency with which scientists during the long formative centuries of Western science said that the task and the reward of the scientist was "to think God's thoughts after him" leads one to believe that this was their real motivation. If so, then modern Western science was cast in a matrix of Christian theology. The dynamism of religious devotion, shaped by the Judeo-Christian dogma of creation, gave it impetus.

AN ALTERNATIVE CHRISTIAN VIEW

We would seem to be headed toward conclusions unpalatable to many Christians. Since both *science* and *technology* are blessed words in our contemporary vocabulary, some may be happy at the notions, first, that, viewed historically, modern science is an extrapolation of natural theology and, second, that modern technology is at least partly to be explained as an Occidental, voluntarist realization of the Christian dogma of man's transcendence of, and rightful mastery over, nature. But, as we now recognize, somewhat over a century ago science and technology —hitherto quite separate activities—joined to give mankind powers which, to judge by many of the ecologic effects, are out of control. If so, Christianity bears a huge burden of guilt.

I personally doubt that disastrous ecologic backlash can be avoided simply by applying to our problems more science and more technology. Our science and technology have grown out of Christian attitudes toward man's relation to nature which are almost universally held not only by Christians and neo-Christians but also by those who fondly regard themselves as post-Christians. Despite Copernicus, all the cosmos rotates around our little globe. Despite Darwin, we are *not,* in our hearts, part of the natural process. We are superior to nature, contemptuous of it, willing to use it for our slightest whim. The newly elected Governor of California, like myself a churchman but less troubled than I, spoke for the Christian tradition when he said (as is alleged), "when you've seen one redwood tree, you've seen them all." To a Christian a tree can be no more than a physical fact. The whole concept of the sacred grove is alien to Christianity and to the ethos of the West. For nearly 2 millennia Christian missionaries have been chopping down sacred groves, which are idolatrous because they assume spirit in nature.

What we do about ecology depends on our ideas of the man-nature relationship. More science and more technology are not going to get us out of the present ecologic crisis until we find a new religion, or rethink our old one. The beatniks, who are the basic revolutionaries of our time, show a sound instinct in their affinity for Zen Buddhism, which conceives of the man-nature relationship as very nearly the mirror image of the Christian view. Zen, however, is as deeply conditioned by Asian history as Christianity is by the experience of the West, and I am dubious of its viability among us.

Possibly we should ponder the greatest radical in Christian history since Christ: Saint Francis of Assisi. The prime miracle of Saint Francis is the fact that he did not end at the stake, as many of his left-wing followers did. He was so clearly heretical that a General of the Franciscan Order, Saint Bonaventura, a great and perceptive Christian, tried to suppress the early accounts of Franciscanism. The key to an understanding of Francis is his belief in the virtue of humility—not merely for the individual but for man as a species. Francis tried to depose man from his monarchy over creation and set up a democracy of all God's creatures. With him the ant is no longer simply a homily for the lazy, flames a sign of the thrust of the soul toward union with God; now they are Brother Ant and Sister Fire, praising the Creator in their own ways as Brother Man does in his.

Later commentators have said that Francis preached to the birds as a rebuke to men who would not listen. The records do not read so: he urged the little birds to praise God, and in spiritual ecstasy they flapped their wings and chirped rejoicing. Legends of saints, especially the Irish saints, had long told of their dealings with animals but always, I believe, to show their human dominance over creatures. With Francis it is different. The land around Gubbio in the Apennines was being ravaged by a fierce wolf. Saint Francis, says the legend, talked to the wolf and persuaded him of the error of his ways. The wolf repented, died in the odor of sanctity, and was buried in consecrated ground.

What Sir Steven Runciman calls "the Franciscan doctrine of the animal soul" was quickly stamped out. Quite possibly it was in part inspired, consciously or unconsciously, by the belief in reincarnation held by the Cathar heretics who at that time teemed in Italy and southern France, and who presumably had got it originally from India. It is significant that at just the same moment, about 1200, traces of metempsychosis are found also in western Judaism, in the Provençal *Cabbala.* But Francis held neither to transmigration of souls nor to pantheism. His view of nature and of man rested on a unique sort of pan-psychism of all things animate and inanimate, designed for the glorification of their transcendent Creator, who, in the ultimate gesture of cosmic humility, assumed flesh, lay helpless in a manger, and hung dying on a scaffold.

I am not suggesting that many contemporary Americans who are concerned about our ecologic crisis will be either able or willing to counsel with wolves or exhort birds. However, the present increasing disruption of the global environment is the product of a dynamic technology and science which were originating in the Western medieval world against which Saint Francis was rebelling in so original a way. Their growth cannot be understood historically apart from distinctive attitudes toward nature which are deeply grounded in Christian dogma. The fact that most people do not think of these attitudes as Christian is irrelevant. No new set of basic values has been accepted in our society to displace those of Christianity. Hence we shall continue to have a worsening ecologic crisis until we reject the Christian axiom that nature has no reason for existence save to serve man.

The greatest spiritual revolutionary in Western history, Saint Francis, proposed what he thought was an alternative Christian view of nature and man's relation to it: he tried to substitute the idea of the equality of all creatures, including man, for the idea of man's limitless rule of creation. He failed. Both our present science and our present technology are so tinctured with orthodox Christian arrogance toward nature that no solution for our ecologic crisis can be expected from them alone. Since the roots of our trouble are so largely religious, the remedy must also be essentially religious, whether we call it that or not. We must rethink and refeel our nature and destiny. The profoundly religious, but heretical, sense of the primitive Franciscans for the spiritual autonomy of all parts of nature may point a direction. I propose Francis as a patron saint for ecologists.

Creation and Environment

JOHN MACQUARRIE

It has been fashionable in recent years among some theologians to make much of the claim that Western science and technology owe their origins to biblical influences, and especially to the biblical doctrine of creation. Among Protestant writers, Harvey Cox has been one of the best-known proponents of this view. The Hebrew understanding of creation, he claims, "separates nature from God." Nature thus becomes "disenchanted" and can be seen in a "matter-of-fact" way. "This disenchantment of the natural world provides an absolute precondition for the development of natural science" and "makes nature itself available for man's use."[1] Among Catholic theologians, Johannes Metz has put forward similar views. He writes: "We could say that where there is no faith in a transcendent Creator, there is also no genuine secularization of the world and no genuine availability of this world to men." He contrasts the Greek view in which God is a kind of immanent principle of the world and

SOURCE: Inaugural lecture as Lady Margaret Professor of Divinity, Oxford University. Subsequently published in *The Expository Times,* 83, no. 1 (October 1971), 4–9. Reprinted by permission of the author and the editor.

1. *The Secular City* (Macmillan, New York, 1965), 22–23.

in which the world therefore retains some kind of numinous quality with the Hebrew view in which the world is entirely external to the creator God and therefore itself "godless," pure world available for man's "active disposing."[2]

That there is a measure of truth in the position advocated by the theologians mentioned need not be denied. But their presentation of it is oversimplified and onesided. Furthermore, some disconcerting conclusions have been drawn from the claims which Cox, Metz and the others have been so anxious to press. It would not be unfair, perhaps, to suppose that at the time when these claims were made the theologians concerned were hoping to re-establish the relevance to the contemporary world of the somewhat faded doctrine of creation and even to gain for it some reflection of the glamour that is popularly ascribed to technology. But in the meanwhile, serious questions have arisen about technology itself. Even in its peaceful applications, it has revealed unsuspected ambiguities. In particular, it has already had such far-reaching effects on the environment that if present trends continue unchecked, man's very survival will be threatened through depletion of resources, overpopulation, pollution of various kinds, health hazards and so on. I do not propose to dwell on dismal matters with which we are all familiar, and I do not wish either to seem unduly pessimistic about the outcome, for man has surmounted many appalling difficulties in the past, and one may hope that he will continue to do the same in the future. But one of the ironies of the new situation is that some secular writers have taken up the theological point that technology has its charter in the Bible and, instead of reckoning this as a credit to the Bible and an illustration of its continuing relevance, have rather blamed the Bible and its doctrine of

2. *Theology of the World* (Herder & Herder, New York, 1969), 65–66.

creation as major factors contributing to the deterioration of the environment. Thus Lynn White, in an essay entitled "The Historical Roots of our Ecologic Crisis," states that "especially in its Western form, Christianity is the most anthropocentric religion the world has ever seen." He points out that in the creation stories of the Bible, everything is planned explicitly for "man's benefit and rule" and that "it is God's will that man exploit nature." As far as our ecological crisis is concerned, he suggests that "Christianity bears a huge burden of guilt."[3] From a different point of view, Max Nicholson makes the charge that "Christianity has signally failed . . . to teach the need for respect towards what it professes to regard as the works of its Creator."[4] Incidentally, both White and Nicholson call for a renewal of the Franciscan elements in the Christian tradition.

While Cox and Metz on the one hand and White and Nicholson on the other differ in their evaluation of the theological doctrine of creation, they are agreed about its profound effects in shaping Western man's attitude toward nature—effects which continue to this day, even if an explicit adherence to the doctrine of creation has been abandoned by large numbers of people. I believe they are correct in thinking that our practical everyday attitudes are influenced by deep-lying convictions of a kind that may be called theological or metaphysical or ontological, and that these may continue to exert an influence in a culture even when they have ceased to be explicit. From this it would follow, however, that any lasting change in practical attitudes, such as might help us to cope better with the problems of environment in a technological era, must be correlated with

3. *The Environmental Handbook,* ed. Garrett de Bell (Ballantine, New York, 1970), 20–23.
4. *The Environmental Revolution* (Hodder & Stoughton, 1970), 265.

a change in our deep convictions (perhaps barely conscious) about man and his relation to the world, for it is from these convictions that our motivations and evaluations proceed.

In saying this, I am agreeing with Lynn White that the problems arising from technology and the environment cannot be solved *only* through the application of more and better technology. Certainly improved technology must be part of the answer, but to suppose that the problems of technology can themselves be solved purely by technology seems to me not only superficial but illogical as well. Herbert Marcuse seems to be much nearer the mark when he declares that we need "a new type of man, a different type of human being, with new needs, capable of finding a qualitatively different way of life, and of constructing a qualitatively different environment."[5] But this seems to me to be a religious demand, for a new type of man emerges only where there are fundamentally new evaluations, and these in turn spring from fundamental convictions of a metaphysical or theological kind. It is at this point that the theologian may make his contribution to the problem—a contribution perhaps no more important but surely no less important than that of the technologists in the various fields. The theologian will make his contribution by looking again to the Christian tradition, by inquiring at what points in the development of that tradition some elements in it came to be distorted through an exaggerated emphasis, and by asking what latent resources remain in the tradition that might respond to the needs of the present situation by introducing correctives and promoting the new attitudes demanded.

I have said that the doctrine found in Metz, Gogarten, Cox

5. *Marxism and Radical Religion,* ed. John C. Raines and Thomas Dean (Temple University Press, Philadelphia, 1970), 7.

and other theologians of recent times that the biblical doctrine of creation provided the charter for Western science and technology is oversimplified and onesided. This becomes apparent if we attend to a few facts which just do not fit the theory. The Hebrews themselves held to a doctrine of creation for several centuries, but they developed no science worth mentioning, and technologically they were inferior to most of the neighbouring peoples in the arts both of peace and war. The science of the ancient world (though, indeed, it was different from modern science) arose among the Greeks for whom God was not a transcendent Creator apart from the world but rather an immanent world Soul. Again, although all Christians have accepted the doctrine of creation, science and technology have not developed equally among them. Early Christianity did not continue the rising science of Greece. Science and technology, as we know them to-day, are a relatively late development in Christendom, and even so they have arisen in Western rather than in Eastern Christianity. So obviously some refinements and distinctions are needed if we are to disentangle the complicated influences that have been at work.

First of all, we may take note that the Hebrew tradition itself is a complex one. It is true that if we confine our attention to the creation stories, we read there of a divine *fiat* which brings into being a world quite external to God the Creator. We read also that man is the primary end of the creation, and that he is commanded to subdue the earth. While man is at the centre of both creation stories, there is a remarkable difference between them. In the older story, the creation of man comes first and the environment is then placed around him. In the later and more sophisticated story, the environment seems to be accorded more importance, for it has to be prepared in successive stages before man appears on the scene. As we go on through the Old Testament, however, we come upon other strains which although never dominant, qualify both the transcendent and the anthropocentric emphases of the creation stories. A notable instance is the covenant which God makes with Noah after the flood. The covenant is made not only with Noah and his descendants, that is to say, with the human race; it is also "with every living creature . . . the birds, the cattle and every beast of the earth."[6] Again, while the Psalms typically celebrate the deeds of the Lord in the history of Israel, some of them frankly delight in the natural world and see God there. "The heavens declare the glory of God. . . ."[7] One commentator says about these words, almost in rebuke, that they "come strangely from the pen of a Hebrew writer,"[8] and he claims that this psalm and others in similar vein have brought in non-Hebrew sources. But surely we should be glad that these foreign elements (if they are foreign) have kept a place in the Old Testament, thereby tempering the notes of transcendence and anthropocentricity that characterize the mainstream of Hebrew thought. Above all, there is the survival of priestly religion alongside the dominant prophetic religion of the Old Testament, and this priestly religion, though overshadowed, had its indispensable rôle. Prophetic religion stresses history against nature and upholds the transcendence and otherness of God. Priestly religion smacks rather of the earthy, the immanent, even the pagan. A contemporary Jewish scholar, Richard Rubinstein, writes: "The priests of ancient Israel wisely never suffered Yahweh entirely to win his war with Baal, Astarte and Anath."[9] Some elements of an earthy, immanent naturalism remained in Hebrew religion, and perhaps

6. Gen 9[10].
7. Ps 19[1].
8. W. O. E. Oesterley, *The Psalms* (S.P.C.K., 1939), vol. I, 168.
9. *After Auschwitz* (Bobbs-Merrill, Indianapolis, 1966), 124.

it still survives at a deep unconscious level and we see a symptom of it in the incredible attachment of the Jews to the soil of Palestine after so many centuries of exile.

Thus the dominant model for understanding the relation of God to the world in the Old Testament is what we may call the monarchical model. God is a self-sufficient and transcendent being who creates the world by an act of will. But, obscure and fragmentary though it may be, there are at least traces of an alternative model, which we may call the organic model. I use this expression to denote a view in which God and the world are not sharply separated.

With the rise of Christianity, the Hebrew heritage was speedily fused with contributions from Greek thought. The idea of God was profoundly affected by these new influences. Since Greek thought itself contained so many strains, it is difficult to say anything briefly about its influence without being guilty of oversimplification. We must remember too that its influence had already been felt in Jewish thought before the emergence of Christianity. It is certainly true that in some forms of Greek philosophy, especially the Platonist tradition, God was conceived as so utterly transcendent in his unchangeable perfection that he was beyond the bounds of speech or thought. In the Stoic tradition, on the other hand, God was an immanent world-principle. But both views differed sharply from what I have called the monarchical model of the dominant Hebrew tradition. In the Greek conception God, even in his transcendence, was a kind of cosmic Absolute, and this favours the organic rather than the monarchical model. The world might be conceived as eternal, and its relation to God understood in terms of emanation rather than of making. Apparently the great Christian thinker Origen took over both of these ideas, though, of course, his teaching was deemed to be heterodox. But even if most Christian thinkers did not go so far as Origen in these matters, the general result of the impact of Greek philosophy was to forge closer bonds between God and nature. An important rôle came to be assigned to natural theology and, even more importantly, to natural law. It was not indeed supposed that God was subject to a natural law more ultimate than himself, but this law was nevertheless supposed to be inherent in the divine nature and not just a product of the divine will. As Paul Tillich has indicated, the impact of Greek rationalism on the early Church was to force it to raise the ontological questions hidden in the personalism of Hebrew religion.[10] As a result, there took place a qualification of the monarchical model of God and its accompanying anthropocentricity, and this meant in turn a higher estimate of nature and world. Perhaps it was the continuance of these ideas in Eastern Christianity which ensured the different attitude to nature which has prevailed there, as Lynn White has suggested. And there are also affinities with the non-Christian religions of the East where, if there is an idea of God, he is conceived more on the organic model.

However, our concern is with the attitudes which have arisen in the West. Long before the secular theologians of recent years had made their claim that science and technology have their origins in the biblical doctrine of creation and certainly long before there was any question of an ecological crisis, Michael B. Foster had published an important article on "The Christian Doctrine of Creation and the Rise of Modern Natural Science."[11] Unlike Christian theologians who have tried to expel from the Christian teaching those elements inherited from

10. *Biblical Religion and the Search for Ultimate Reality* (University of Chicago Press, 1955), 5 ff.
11. *Mind*, vol. xliii (1934). Reprinted in *Creation: The Impact of an Idea*, ed. D. O'Connor and F. Oakley (Scribner, New York, 1969), 29 ff.

Greece in favour of what they would like to consider a purely biblical and revealed faith, Foster was quite clear that a balanced Christianity needs the contribution of the Greeks as well as that of the Hebrews. Concerning the Christian doctrine of creation, he wrote: "The Christian doctrine on this, as on all other subjects, itself includes an element derived from Greek philosophy, and any doctrine from which all Greek elements are excluded is less than Christian."[12] He was also clearer than some of the secularizing theologians that the rise of science needed not only a doctrine of creation but a knowledge of mathematics. Obviously we did not get that from the Bible, and perhaps the lack of it accounts for the absence of any science among the ancient Hebrews. But Foster's analysis also shows that from a very early time there was a drive within Christendom to rid Christian doctrine of Greek influences and to return to a pure biblicism, and especially to the monarchical model of God. This drive, taking elements of Greek rationalism with it and combining them with an extreme Hebrew voluntarism, made possible the harnessing of science to technology and the transformation of the environment that has come about in the modern world. The ancient Greek science, of course, was pursued without much regard to its practical applications.

We see the attempt to expel Greek influences already in the later Middle Ages. Among the Scotists, natural law in the organic sense gave way to a law based purely on the will of God, while the Occamists rejected natural theology to rely on revelation alone. These tendencies reached their most extreme form in Calvinism. The sovereignty of God is the key doctrine of the Calvinist system and the monarchical model of God receives uncompromising expression. Everything happens by the divine

12. *Loc. cit.*, *52.*

will. The world itself is a product of a free act of God's will, and he might equally well have refrained from creating, so that in no sense is the world organic to God. There is a continuous line from Calvin to our own time, to Barth, Gogarten, Brunner and finally the secular theologians who have pushed Barthianism to its conclusions. In spite of some fine insights which he achieved in his book, *Christianity and Civilization,* Brunner has given one of the most extreme statements of that utter devaluation and profanation of the physical world which seems to follow from regarding it as a more or less arbitrary product of the divine will, entirely separated from God. He put this statement in the form of two equations:

God minus the world = God
The world minus God = Zero

This may be pure biblical theology, purified of all Greek influences. But it seems also to be an acosmism, and perhaps expresses also an unconscious egotistic will to power. Concerning the doctrine that the world is the product of divine will and nothing in itself, Ludwig Feuerbach wrote: "In the inmost depths of thy soul, thou wouldest rather there were no world, for where the world is, there is matter, and where there is matter there is weight and resistance, space and time, limitation and necessity. Nevertheless, there *is* a world and there *is* matter. How dost thou escape from the dilemma of this contradiction? How dost thou expel the world from thy consciousness, that it may not disturb thee in the beatitude of the unlimited soul? Only by making the world itself a product of will, by giving it an arbitrary existence, always hovering between existence and non-existence, always awaiting its annihilation."[13] And if it is this

13. *The Essence of Christianity* (Harper & Row, New York, 1957), 110.

acosmic or even anti-cosmic attitude that has led us to exploit with recklessness and indifference the resources of the world and to subject science increasingly to the service of acquisitive ends, then indeed Lynn White's accusation would stand—that Christianity, or, at least, one influential form of it, bears a huge burden of guilt for some of our present troubles.

Of course, it must be acknowledged that even in Western Christianity there have been other ways of understanding the meaning of creation and these have conduced to better practical attitudes to the world. I have mentioned already that both White and Nicholson commend St. Francis for his sense of affinity with the whole creation. A later example is Luther, who believed that because the world is God's creation, even the meanest objects in nature have some dignity and interest. To mention his own homely example, he says that God is present in a louse's belly. One might contrast this with the obvious contempt shown by Aristophanes for the alleged investigations by Socrates into such humble creatures as fleas and gnats: "Thrice happy Socrates! It would not be difficult to succeed in a law suit, knowing so much about a gnat's guts!"[14] Karl Jaspers is a modern philosopher who has taken up the view that the Christian doctrine of creation has conferred upon everyday objects an interest which they did not have for the Greeks. But while there are some evidences to support this view, I believe that for the majority the doctrine of voluntary creation has led to depriving the world of intrinsic interest and to seeing it primarily in a utilitarian way as an object for exploitation, which the Greeks did not. Still another idea that has sometimes gained currency is that of stewardship. Belief in a Creator, it is said, implies that the world is not placed at man's absolute disposal,

14. *The Clouds,* 167–168.

for he is accountable to God. Unfortunately, however, the notion of a transcendent God who hands over the world to men can often develop into a kind of deism in which this distant God who started things off has pretty well bowed himself out of the picture, and then there is not much validity left to the notion of stewardship. I think this has happened in some versions of secular theology which stress man's coming of age and his taking over of the world. Nevertheless, there are still some attempts at a rehabilitation of the stewardship idea. Hugh Montefiore, one of the few Christian writers who has tried to face the theological issues raised by the ecological crisis, has rightly seen that "what is needed is . . . a redirection of inward attitudes,"[15] and he believes that this might be achieved through a better awareness of our responsibility as stewards of the creation. I believe that the notion of responsibility is of the greatest importance in this connexion, but whether a doctrine of stewardship can support it is more doubtful, for in such a doctrine, as it seems to me, the world is still considered as a piece of property and primarily from an anthropocentric angle. Least hopeful of all is still another attitude which sometimes clothes itself with religious phraseology—a kind of nostalgic, sentimental conservationism. This attitude is frequently hypocritical as well, as when Americans and Europeans who enjoy the affluence of technological civilization urge upon Africans or Asians the duty of keeping their forest lands in the unspoiled state in which God had created them. If this means a continuing marginal existence for the peoples of these lands, except for the occasional crumbs that might fall from the picnic tables of vacationing tourists from the West, then the plea is likely to go unheard, and deservedly so.

In all parts of the world, science and technology will—if no

15. *Can Man Survive?* (Collins, 1970), 53.

unforeseen calamities occur—continue to advance, and so will the industrialization and urbanization that accompany them. I do not think we would have it otherwise, and even if we did, I do not think we could reverse the process, for these things have acquired a certain momentum. But it becomes increasingly important to control the process, to set limits to the exploitation of nature, to become sensitive to those points at which, in damaging his environment, man is also damaging himself, not only physically but also mentally and spiritually. With technology as with so much else, we have still to learn the truth of that ancient piece of moral wisdom, μηδὲν ἄγαν, nothing too much.

We have, however, seen reason to believe that we shall not learn this truth unless there takes place a very profound change in our basic beliefs, so far as these shape our attitude toward the physical environment. As far as Christian theology is concerned, my thesis is that we need to move away from the monarchical model of God toward the organic model. The monarchical model is deeply entrenched in much traditional Christian language, including the language of liturgy, it is widespread in popular theology, and it is encouraged also by those forms of biblical theology which try to exclude all philosophical influences and to found themselves on revelation alone. On the other hand, as the crisis in theism in the past few years has shown, the monarchical model of God has become increasingly less credible to many people to-day. The organic model, by contrast, has gained ground in philosophical theology, and I think most philosophical versions of theism to-day, even those that proceed from very different schools, are of the organic type.[16] They seek to recover what was of value in the non-Hebraic elements of the Christian tradition, and especially the

16. I have in mind such diverse thinkers as Hartshorne and Tillich.

affinity between God and the world in opposition to the sharp separation of God and world. Of course, there is no attempt to isolate these elements. Rather, they have to be integrated into the mainstream thought of God, but when this happens, they profoundly qualify the monarchical model of God in the direction of the organic model.

If we go back to Brunner's two equations, mentioned earlier, organic theism has no difficulty in accepting one of them, namely, that without God, without the creative Spirit, the world ceases to exist. But it denies the other equation, namely, that without the world, God is still God, as if quite unaffected in his majesty and self-sufficiency. For if God is indeed creative Spirit, then his creation cannot be a mere arbitrary product of will, so that he might either have created or not created, or so that he would be unaffected by the absence of a creation. This does not mean that he *needs* to create, but it does mean that it is his nature *as God* to create. There is an analogy with natural law, which does not *bind* God, but *flows* from him. Thus the world is organically related to God. He expresses himself in the world and even puts himself in the world—an idea which should be readily acceptable to Christianity as *par excellence* the religion of incarnation. To put the matter in another way, the monarchical model sees the relation of God to the world as completely asymmetrical; the organic model sees this relation as at least in some respects a symmetrical one. God not only affects the world but is affected by it, even limited by it. Hence this view also allows far more for the possibility of a tragic element in creation. What chiefly concerns us, however, is that the organic model of theism and of creation allows to the world a dignity and even a mystery that it could not have on the monarchical model. The world is understood as organic to God, not as a mere product of his will. This means also that the world cannot be conceived in narrowly anthropocentric terms, as if it were provided solely for man's exploitation.

If, as Christian theologians rethink the meaning of theism, the organic model becomes more influential, as it seems likely to do, then I think this will promote better attitudes toward the physical environment and will perhaps in some measure atone for excesses which in the past may have been encouraged by the dominance of the monarchical view. But a final question remains to trouble us. Is it not perhaps too late for this theological rethinking to take place? I do not mean too late in the sense that the ecological crisis is so pressing that there is no time left for the reshaping of our attitudes before the day of reckoning arrives, though that, unfortunately, may be true. I mean rather that it may be too late for any theological model to have an influence because of the decline of theology and the secularization of our outlook. Is either a monarchical or an organic model of God's relation to the world of any relevance when many people have come to think of God himself as a projection of man? Perhaps two answers can be given to this question. The first is that the theological understanding of these matters has still a considerable influence, more possibly than is commonly allowed, and that in any case the theologian does have a duty to address himself to the problems vexing our time and to make what contribution he can from his resources. The second answer is that the position of the humanist may not be so very different, and that he too has to choose between different models. I think it would be true to say that there is a monarchical type of humanism and an organic type. The monarchical type makes man the measure of all things and sets the world over against him as his object. This is the type which would maintain that the problem of technology and environment must be seen as itself a purely technological problem, or a series of such problems. The organic type of humanism is much more aware of man's affinity with the world and recognizes that he is part of something much bigger than he has yet understood and to which he owes a responsibility as yet undefined. Since the theist believes that man is made in God's image, then an organic type of theism and an organic type of humanism have some kinship. On the basis of this kinship, they can work together to build up a better and more responsible attitude toward the environment, and so play some part in enabling man to survive the dangers which threaten him.

Man and Nature: The Ecological Controversy and the Old Testament

JAMES BARR

It is hardly necessary for me to inform this audience that we live in a time of controversy about ecology, about the balance of the natural environment in which man lives. The subject has sprung into increasing prominence in the last decade or so, and now hardly a day passes without revelations of the danger threatened to our natural resources and our future life by toxic wastes, by ill-used pesticides, by all kinds of pollution of land, sea and air. This phenomenon is not entirely new; the industrial landscape of much of the north of England is an instance close to us at this moment, and much of it goes back to the older industrial revolution of the eighteenth and nineteenth centuries. But in recent years the problem has become much more acute, because our technology can upset the balance of nature more profoundly than the older forms of waste or exploitation did. At the same time scientific knowledge makes us more aware of the danger. Politicians are becoming more conscious of the matter, and it is likely that the control of pollution and the protection of the

SOURCE: A lecture delivered in the John Rylands Library, Manchester, England, 1972. Subsequently published in the *Bulletin of the John Rylands Library,* 55, no. 1 (Autumn 1972), 9–32. Reprinted by permission of the author and the Library.

environment will be a main centre of social and ethical discussion in the next decades.

This present lecture, however, is not concerned primarily with the political, social and technical possibilities, though it may have some connection with them. What interests me specifically is the relation between the ecological controversy on the one hand and on the other the Jewish-Christian religious tradition, with its foundation in the Bible and particularly in the Old Testament.[1] It has been argued that religious currents of thought have in fact contributed to the origin and history of the present problem; and, conversely, those who stand within the Jewish and Christian religious tradition may be forced by the modern ecological discussion to take a fresh look at certain aspects of their own belief and to reconsider the biblical background of it.

Now to the average intelligent person it may be far from immediately clear what the Bible has to do with the pollution of the environment. What direct connection is there between the Old Testament, of which the manuscript and early printed evidence is so richly exemplified in this distinguished library, and the undrinkability of the water of the Irwell, only a few minutes' walk away? Well, there is a theory which connects the two, and which will be basic to the discussion of this lecture. It goes as follows:

First of all, modern science ultimately rests upon a founda-

1. Publications on the subject have been multiplying fast. Among those which have taken an interest in the religious aspect of it I would mention H. Montefiore, *Can Man Survive?* (Fontana, 1969); J. Black, *The Dominion of Man: The Search for Ecological Responsibility* (Edinburgh, 1970); *Man in His Living Environment* (Church of England Information Office); "God in Nature and History," an ecumenical report, basically by H. Berkhof, published in *New Directions in Faith and Order: Bristol 1967* (World Council of Churches, Geneva, 1968), pp. 7–31. This lecture was already complete when I came across J. Macquarrie, "Creation and Environment," *Expository Times,* lxxxiii (1971–2), 4–9.

tion provided by the Bible. The doctrine of creation, as seen especially in the Genesis story, made an essential separation between God and the world. In many religions nature, or some aspect of nature, is somehow divine or partakes in divinity; in the biblical religion, on the contrary, nature is "de-divinized."[2] On the other hand, though nature is something other than God, it is explicit in Genesis that nature is not anti-God; it is not something opposed to God, something in itself evil. On the contrary, as Genesis puts it, "God saw that it was good"; and according to Genesis the created world is a cosmos, an ordered whole. Modern science did not originate within the biblical experience, but nevertheless some basis derived from the biblical experience was necessary in order that the later scientific world-outlook might arise. It could not, according to the theory I am describing, have arisen in a world where nature was regarded either as partaking in the divine or as partaking in evil. It is characteristic therefore that science arose within a Western and Christian culture; and, even though scientists commonly do not recognize it, it is from the demythologization of the world in the Book of Genesis that science ultimately in a historical sense derives.

There is another aspect to this same theory. The biblical religion, it points out, set man over nature and gave him authority, indeed encouragement, to govern and control it. In Genesis man is the crown of the creative process; he is in the image of God and thus sharply distinguished from the remainder of the creaturely world. He is told by God to "have dominion" over the animals, to "subdue" the earth. Scientific technology is the fullest development of this controlling status of mankind. It is

2. The German phrase, "die Entgötterung der Natur," expresses the idea somewhat more gracefully; I do not know who first used it.

not only a study of what goes on in nature, it is also a taking of control. Technology can thus be thought of as a sort of secular fulfilment of a basic outlook about humanity which was already expressed in Genesis.

In these respects, then, it is argued, modern science, in spite of its own frequently irreligious form, stands in some considerable harmony with the biblical and Hebraic attitude to the world. It correspondingly contrasts with the Greek attitude. Though the ancient Greeks did develop the sciences in some degree, science in its modern form could not have arisen on the soil of Greek thinking. It was the heritage of Aristotle above all that had to be shaken off at the Renaissance and Reformation before modern science could be free to progress. This point indeed contains the answer offered to one of the obvious objections which might be made against the entire theory we are considering. It might be asked: if modern science has its basis in the biblical world-view, why then did it not take its rise until many centuries after the biblical heritage in Christianity had become culturally dominant in the world? The answer commonly given is somewhat as follows: during the Middle Ages the Church in Western Europe "saw it as her duty to preserve and develop the Graeco-Roman scientific heritage, embodied in works such as those of Ptolemy of Alexandria. This was a heritage of static conceptions about nature and history."[3] It is represented, then, that the Jewish-Christian religious tradition, at least if properly understood, is favourable towards science, while the Greek tradition is unfavourable.

You will notice that I bracket "Jewish" and "Christian" together as one element. Of course the civilization in which modern science grew up was a Western and Christian one, and

3. So "God in Nature and History," op. cit. p. 16.

Judaism was a minority religion in it; for its basic conceptions of man and the world, however, Christianity went back to the Old Testament, and for all purposes of argument in this lecture Judaism and Christianity can be taken together, even though some writers may mention only one of them.

Indeed there has been a tendency to include along with Judaism and Christianity also the case of Islam; for Islam also is a religion of the same group, with its origin on Semitic soil; and those whose theory we are discussing seem often to make favourable mention of Muslim science, and of its part in bridging the gap between antiquity and science in its modern form.

Incidentally, the favourable mention of Muslim science in this connection is one of the curiosities of the whole theory. It is difficult to find in print an explicit statement of what is meant, but probably the usual opinion is somewhat as follows: such scientific progress as there was during the Middle Ages did not take place in Europe, where it was stifled by Aristotelianism and the Greek heritage in general. It took place in the Islamic world, and this belongs rather to the circle of revelation along with Judaism and Christianity, going back basically to the Bible in its ideas of man and nature. If this is what has been meant, however, the argument is a poor one, for the main content and attitudes of Islamic science appear to derive solidly from Greek sources.[4] Within the context of the present discussion, the case

4. Cf. for example these two quotations from *The Legacy of Islam* (ed. Arnold and Guillaume, Oxford, 1931): in "Science and Medicine," p. 354, M. Meyerhof writes: "Looking back we may say that Islamic medicine and science reflected the light of the Hellenic sun, when its day had fled"; and in "Astronomy and Mathematics," p. 376, Carra de Vaux writes: "The Arabs are before all else the pupils of the Greeks: their science is a continuation of Greek science which it preserves, cultivates, and on a number of important points develops and perfects." See now also F. Rosenthal, *Das Fortleben der Antike im Islam* (Zurich and Stuttgart, 1965).

of Muslim science must logically lead in a direction opposite to that in which it is commonly supposed to lead.

To return to our main topic, the interpretation which I have been expounding is one which establishes a sort of inner unity between natural science and Jewish-Christian faith, at least in its biblical form. It accepts with satisfaction the progress of science and technology, and argues that biblical religion has been an important factor in enabling man to stand over against nature and so eventually to dominate it. The conflicts between science and religion, so marked in the nineteenth century, were superficial rather than profound; they were caused largely by the failure of religious people either to understand their own biblical and theological tradition or to discern the true nature and value of the scientific progress that was being made.

It may well be asked who are the people who have in fact held and made popular this doctrine. Like a number of ideas which have become part of the stock-in-trade of current theology, it is not always easy to discover who first propounded it or to find an exposition of it which is both typical on the one hand and careful and competent on the other. Great influence was certainly exercised by three articles of M. B. Foster in 1934–6.[5] These argue that there are "un-Greek elements" in the modern theory of nature and that the peculiar character of the modern science of nature has been determined by these; the source of these un-Greek elements is the Christian doctrine of creation.[6] Foster's argument, however, is neither biblicistic nor anti-Greek; he does not lay stress on Hebrew thinking (cf. *Mind,* xliii, 465, n. 1), and he regards the Christian doctrine of creation as having derived a great deal from the Greek. His arguments

5. *Mind,* N.S., xliii (1934), 446–68; xliv (1935), 439–66; xlv (1936), 1–27.
6. *Mind,* xliii. 448.

receive considerable attention from theologians like John Baillie[7] and E. L. Mascall.[8] Baillie cites the Russian thinker Berdyaev as asserting that "Christianity alone made possible both positive science and technics"[9] and the philosopher John Macmurray as claiming that modern science is not only "the product of Christianity" but "its most adequate expression so far."[10] Works which later popularized this sort of position, like Alan Richardson in his *The Bible in the Age of Science* (London, 1961), are more anti-Greek.[11]

A full statement of our theory, in a strongly Hebraic dress, comes from Harvey Cox in his well-known book *The Secular City* (London, 1965). The Hebrew view of creation is a marked departure from previously existing world-views. "It separates nature from God and distinguishes man from nature." This is a process whereby nature becomes, in Cox's term, "disenchanted"; and this "allows man to perceive nature itself in a matter-of-fact way." "This disenchantment of the natural world provides an absolute precondition for the development of natural science."[12]

In any case, I believe that opinions of this type about the relation between science and Jewish-Christian faith have become very common, and can only agree with Prof. Macquarrie in his opening sentence: "It has been fashionable in recent years among some theologians to make much of the claim that Western science and technology owe their origins to biblical influ-

7. *Natural Science and the Spiritual Life* (Oxford, 1951).
8. *Christian Theology and Natural Science* (London, 1956); cf. pp. 94 ff.
9. *The Meaning of History* (London, 1936); cf. Baillie, p. 30.
10. *The Clue to History* (London, 1938); cf. Baillie, p. 31.
11. Cf. the account of "Greek pseudo-science," pp. 14–16.
12. Cox, pp. 22–24. I have not been able to see the similar work of the Roman Catholic theologian J. Metz, *Theology of the World,* cited by Macquarrie, op. cit. p. 4.

ences, and especially to the biblical doctrine of creation."

Now this interpretation of which we have been speaking not only makes a connection between natural science on the one side and the biblical and Jewish-Christian tradition on the other, but also attaches a high positive value to this connection. Science and technology are highly valued within it, and the association of the Bible with them is understood to redound to the credit of the Bible. It might be unfair to suggest that this is a mere piece of apologetics, an attempt to gain for biblical religion some reflection of the prestige attaching to science; but though this was not the intention of those who framed this theory, in the result it may have had very much this effect on those who accepted it.[13] In it the achievements of science and technology are very positively valued, and the relation between science and biblical faith serves to shed some reflected value upon the latter.

In the last few years, however, this rather sunny and positive account of the relation between science and biblical faith has begun to be countered by a darker and more negative one. The difference lies in whether we are looking at the achievements of science or at the dangers brought upon us by technology. If science is related to biblical faith, then the achievements of science may be made to redound to the credit of biblical faith; but by the same argument the pollution crisis and the dangers of damaging the environment can be taken as a discreditable consequence of faults and weaknesses in Jewish-Christian faith. In 1967 Lynn White, Jr., a professor of history in Los Angeles, published in the American weekly *Science* an article called "The Historical Roots of our Ecologic Crisis."[14] He argued that the

13. Macquarrie, op. cit. p. 4, does consider it fair to say that the theologians concerned "were hoping . . . even to gain for it [i.e. the doctrine of creation] some reflection of the glamour that is popularly ascribed to technology."
14. *Science,* 155, 10 March 1967, no. 3767, pp. 1203–7.

ecological crisis was unintelligible without an understanding of its religious background; and mere technological advances, he suggested, could not be expected to solve it without a revolution in religious attitudes at the same time. Christianity, he maintained, is much to blame for the existence of the present crisis. "Christianity . . . not only established a dualism of man and nature but also insisted that it is God's will that man exploit nature for his proper ends." And, again, "By destroying pagan animism, Christianity made it possible to exploit nature in a mood of indifference to the feelings of natural objects." Thus "Christianity bears a huge burden of guilt," for our science and technology are deeply "tinctured with orthodox Christian arrogance toward nature."

The difference between the argument we have already described and the position of Lynn White is one of emphasis between positive and negative. The idea of the relation between biblical faith and modern science is the same in both. But while this has generally been given a positive evaluation, White speaks in terms not of praise but of blame. For him, this is Christian arrogance; for him, the command of Genesis that man should dominate the earth is not at all a good thing. While the main theological tradition, in linking biblical faith with the rise of science, has basically claimed that the biblical tradition in this respect was entirely right, White is already looking in another direction. The connection between biblical faith and modern science and technology is a good reason why we should revolt against biblical faith. Along with some of the hippy culture, he recognizes Buddhism as a possible option; but he himself in the end turns to St. Francis who, he maintains, "proposed what he thought was an alternative Christian view of nature and man's relation to it; he tried to substitute the idea of the equality of all creatures, including man, for the idea of man's limitless rule of creation."

According to this newer view, then, the ecological crisis reveals a profound fault in the Jewish-Christian religious tradition. It is likely, moreover, that this point of view will be widely influential. Lynn White's article was widely excerpted and reprinted in magazines like *Horizon* (summer 1967). In general, many of the valuable works now being published on ecology make some comment on the relations of the subject to religion. Not all of them, however, do this in the same way. Max Nicholson maintains that "organised religion" is the chief obstacle standing in the way of a harmony between man and nature.[15] In this respect ancient Judaism and modern Christianity are particularly bad, for they preach "man's unqualified right of dominance over nature." One might just conceivably find in the Old Testament some limited qualifications to man's ruthlessness; but any such restraints "are feeble compared with its chronic and uninhibited incitement towards aggressive, exploitative and reproductively irresponsible behavior in the human species." The churches, Nicholson argues, should have rethought the whole matter in the light of modern experience, but have abysmally failed to do so;[16] "their adherents have, with few exceptions, persisted in behaving as rampant Old Testament tribes."

Again, Jean Dorst in the foreword to his book makes a contrast between "Oriental philosophies" and "Western philosophies," and says that the latter "emphasize the supremacy of man over the rest of creation, which exists only to serve him"; and in illustration of this he cites Genesis i. 28–29.[17] Dorst,

15. *The Environmental Revolution* (London, 1970), pp. 264 f. It is not quite clear whether Nicholson either knows or, like Lynn White, accepts the theory we have been describing, i.e. the view that the intellectual roots of science and technology lie in the biblical religion. His thinking seems to lie rather on the level of popular ideas of the Old Testament as a crude and violent work.
16. It is not clear whether Nicholson has any knowledge of reports by official church bodies, such as those mentioned in n. 1, p. 49, above.
17. *Before Nature Dies* (London, 1970), pp. 18 f.

however—and here, I submit, he is much more fair than Nicholson—points out that quite similar tendencies can be found in materialist philosophies, so that a failure to emphasize the protection of animals and plants is not peculiar to the religions but belongs in general to "the European philosophy whence our technical civilization was derived."

All such arguments are likely in the next decades to form a significant challenge to Jewish and Christian religion. One more reason for this which we may add is that they follow the same lines as an older and more familiar argument, which was not about science and technology but about capitalism.[18] According to this view, capitalism was engendered by Calvinistic and puritanic (i.e. highly biblical) types of religion; and, in the context of the argument, capitalism is essentially an exploitative process directed towards the means of industrial production, just as the ecological crisis derives from exploitative processes towards nature itself. Echoes of that older discussion are likely to be heard within the newer; and in both cases, it will be suggested by some, Jewish-Christian biblical faith is seen to encourage in people an irresponsible exploitative urge.

Such then is the setting of the matter in present-day discussion and, given that this is so, I propose to look at Genesis, and the Old Testament as a whole once again, and to consider whether in this whole matter it has been rightly used. Naturally I am not so naive as to suppose that the Book of Genesis can settle our technological problems of today; and no one, I think, supposes that it can. I am concerned with the historical question, whether the connections which have been established between the Bible and modern science or technology are the result

18. See, among the multitude of literature, M. Weber, *The Protestant Ethic and the Spirit of Capitalism* (1930); R. H. Tawney, *Religion and the Rise of Capitalism* (1926); K. Samuelsson, *Religion and Economic Action* (New York, 1961).

of fair interpretation of its interests and tendencies, and whether the Bible really has in the history of ideas a connection with science and technology of the kind which I have described.

Now, to begin by stating my own opinion in general, I would submit that the whole connection set up between the Bible and modern science and technology, as described earlier in this lecture, is thoroughly faulty and needs to be entirely rethought. As we have seen, Lynn White, in blaming the Jewish-Christian tradition for the ecological crisis, predicated his assertions on the same position which theologians had argued in order to associate that tradition with the origins of modern science.[19] The theologians cannot expect to escape from the censure of Lynn White unless they abandon or revise the set of hypothetical connections in the history of ideas upon which he and they alike depend. In order to do this, one need not argue that there is no connection between the Jewish-Christian doctrine of creation, or its biblical foundations, and the rise of science or the assumptions of science. Science did in fact grow up in a Jewish-Christian world, and the doctrines and legends of that world had an enormous influence on everything that went on in that world. But to suppose that these doctrines not only influenced the rise of science but had an extremely vital and preponderating causal relation to it, seems just enormously improbable.[20] In saying this I am encouraged by

19. Within Lynn White's work one cannot help contrasting the generality and vagueness of his article in *Science* which, as I have said, depends upon the same general theory as many theologians hold, and the precision and carefully evidenced nature of his own expert work *Medieval Technology and Social Change* (Oxford, 1962).

20. Careful theologians, aware of the weakness of the position under discussion, often have to phrase it negatively; thus Archbishop Temple wrote: "It may be too much to argue, as some students of the subject have done, that science is a fruit of Christianity, but it may be safely asserted that it can never spontaneously grow up in regions where the ruling principle of the Universe is believed to be either capricious or hostile"—see J. D. Davies, *Beginning Now* (London, 1971), p. 124. Negative arguments of this kind, or similarly the argument that ancient Indian metaphysics never produced any scientific research, do not in fact prove much.

the fact that, though many theologians confidently assert such a relation, historians of science appear to be able to do much of their work without even mentioning it,[21] and most men of science, I would suspect, would be very surprised to hear that any such opinion existed at all.[22]

The relations between Genesis, its later interpretations in Jewish-Christian doctrine, and the origins of science and technology seem to me to be far different in character. I shall begin with some points in the interpretation of Genesis and return to the broader issues later.

Firstly, what is the image of God in man? Since the collapse of the older orthodox Christian exegesis, according to which the image consisted in the spirituality of man, his soul or his rationality, the dominant tendency has been to identify the image as being man's position of dominion over nature—which, after all, occurs in the very same passage. As God governs all, so man in the image of God governs the remainder of creation: an analogical relation.[23] But I do not think that this is a probable exegesis. As I have argued elsewhere,[24] the passage is concerned with a long-standing, and peculiarly Israelite, debate about the question of likeness between God and man; it is within that context

21. Thus H. Butterfield, who is certainly sensitive to theological questions, appears to have written his *The Origins of Modern Science,* covering the crucial period 1300–1800, without any mention of the said relation.

22. Their surprise would be shared by the vast majority of adherents of the Christian and Jewish faiths, who are totally unaware of this relation; its existence is in fact very much an esoteric belief of theologians.

23. Cf. for instance "God in Nature and History," op. cit. p. 18: "When Gen. i. 27 says that God created man in his own image, the whole passage i. 26–28 makes it clear that what is mainly thought of is man's dominion over nature. As God is the Lord over his whole creation, so he elects man as his representative to exercise this lordship in God's name over the lower creation."

24. See my "The Image of God in the Book of Genesis—A Study of Terminology," *Bulletin of the John Rylands Library,* li (1968–9), 11–26. . . .

that the terms like "image" and "likeness" make sense. The point was not that man had a likeness to God through acting as God's representative towards the rest of created nature, but that he himself was like God. In what way he was like God is not stated; probably it was essential to the writer's position that it could not be stated. There is of course a connection between the image and the dominion over nature, but this is not such that the image consisted in the dominion. It is likely rather to be a consequential relation: *since* man is in the image of God, let him have dominion, etc. Negatively, we may note one additional point. The idea that the image consists in dominion over nature does not fit with the other two places at which the image terminology is used, namely Genesis v. 3 ("Adam had a son in his own image") and ix. 6 ("he that sheds the blood of man, by man shall his blood be shed, because in the image of God he created man"). Homicide was to be punished not because man had dominion over the animals, but because man was like God. In general, then, though man's dominion over the rest of the world is connected with his being created in the image of God, this is not the essential point of the image; and any exegesis which so interprets has the effect of laying too strong an emphasis on this dominion. The dominion over nature remains in any case a fact within the text, but it has come to be over-emphasized in that trend of exegesis which has made it identical with the image of God in man.

Secondly, then, turning to the subject of man's dominion, the emphasis in Genesis does not appear to lie on man's power or on his exploitative activities. There has indeed been in the modern exegetical tradition, especially when the image of God has been identified with man's dominion over the world, a tendency to dwell with some satisfaction on the *strength* of the terms employed.[25] Thus it is argued that the verb *rada* "have dominion" is used physically of the treading or trampling of the winepress; and the verb *kabaš* "subdue" means "stamp down." According to Black (p. 37), it "is elsewhere used for the military subjugation of conquered territory, and clearly implies reliance on force"; it "is a very powerful expression of man's attitude to the rest of nature, and suggests that he sees himself in a position of absolute command."

There are, however, elements which indicate that the matter is not one of simple power or exploitation. A point of general structural importance is the fact that the most obvious of all human relationships to the animals, i.e. the use of animal flesh for food, does not here come into consideration. Genesis i is explicit that in the beginning man was vegetarian, as were also the animals; the only difference was that man ate one element of the vegetation and the animals another. In the P source of the Pentateuch—the same source as Genesis i—the authority for the eating of animal flesh is quite expressly given only after the Deluge, Genesis ix. 2–3 (NEB: "Every creature that lives and moves shall be food for you; I give you them all, as once I gave you all green plants"). Similarly, it is only at this point that we hear that human domination might produce any kind of unpleasant consequences for the animal world. In ix. 1 there is repeated the command "Be fruitful and increase, and fill the earth," as in Genesis i; but here it is followed, as is not the case there, with the assertion that "the fear and terror of you shall be upon all the beasts of the earth." Thus the human "domin-

25. See for instance von Rad, *Genesis* (1961), p. 58; *Old Testament Theology,* i. 146; Black, *Dominion of Man,* p. 37. Black's fine book—not by an Old Testament scholar—suffers somewhat from dependence at such points on a rather narrow line of exegesis (e.g. dependence on Cassuto; Black, op. cit. pp. 35 f.).

ion" envisaged by Genesis i included no idea of using the animals for meat and no terrifying consequences for the animal world. Human exploitation of animal life is not regarded as an inevitable part of human existence, as something given and indeed encouraged by the ideal conditions of the original creation; at most, it is something that comes along later, after a deterioration in the human condition, as a kind of second-best. This fact makes a very considerable difference to the total impact of the idea of human dominion within the legends of Genesis.

All this leads us to look once again at the two verbs *rada* "have dominion" and *kabaš* "subdue," of which so many exegetes have remarked that they are "very strong." Of *rada* we should not attach much importance to the physical sense "tread out (the wine-press)" (only Joel iv. 13, *bo'u rᵉdu*); even granting that this is the same verb, it is quite another semantic department of it. We should not allow the physical sense to dominate over general usage just because physical senses are "primary." The word means "govern, rule, have dominion," and is used quite generally of kings ruling over certain areas, of masters controlling servants, of God ruling his land, ruling in the midst of his enemies, and so on. For instance, in I Kings v. 4 (EV iv. 24) the verb is used to express Solomon's dominion (expressly a peaceful dominion) over a wide area. The word is not at all necessarily a "strong" one (NEB at I Kings iv. 24 well renders "he was paramount").

The other verb, *kabaš* "subdue," has a better claim to be regarded as "strong"; it can be said to suggest violent physical movements like trampling down. But here another difference comes in: this word is not used of the animals but only of the earth, in our passage "fill up the earth and subdue it." I doubt whether more is intended here than the basic needs of settlement and agriculture: man is to fill up the earth, take possession of it, and take control of it. Basically what is intended is tilling; it corresponds with the "working" or "tilling" of the ground in the J story, Genesis ii. 5, 15.

What then is the basic interest of Genesis in the whole matter of the animals in their relation to man? Why should the matter have attracted the concern of the writer in the first place? The most natural view, I would suggest, is that this is a paradise picture. It narrates for the beginning of the world a situation very similar to that which Isaiah xi relates for a future time, namely a period when there is peace in the animal world, peace between animal and man, no eating of animal flesh either by man or by animal, and the whole idyllic scene presided over by man. Man's "dominion" therefore contains no markedly exploitative aspect; it approximates to the well-known Oriental idea of the Shepherd King. The corresponding element in the J story is the point at which God brings the animals (as partners!) to the first man "to see what he would call them" (ii. 19).

We can thus expect that exegetes will in the future tend to reduce their emphasis on the "strength" of the terminology for man's dominion over nature in Genesis. Such a tendency is already visible in the fine commentary of C. Westermann, now appearing in the series Biblischer Kommentar. He points out that the use of *rada* "have dominion, govern" in i. 26 can be compared with what is said in i. 16 about the sun and moon, which are to "govern" the day and night (a different Hebrew word indeed, but there is no reason to suppose that this makes much difference).[26] Westermann writes that this is *herrschen, beherrschen* in the wider sense, as found in German when one speaks *von einer die Landschaft beherrschenden Höhe* ("of a high point dominating the landscape") or *von vorherrschenden*

26. Westermann, *Genesis*, pp. 219 f., 183.

Einflüssen ("of predominating influences"). The sense "govern" is *uneigentlich,* not the proper one; there is no idea of exploitation, and man would lose his "royal" position in the realm of living things if the animals were to him an object of use or of prey.

It is of course possible to argue that the Genesis account of creation has had an influence on the growth of science and technology not through its own original meaning but through the interpretations which have been placed upon it. It would then be possible that, even if the original sense as I suggest laid little stress upon exploitation, nevertheless the general effect of the passage in the history of ideas had been one which encouraged ideas of human force and exploitation. This may or may not be so; I have not been able to carry out a study of the ways in which Genesis in this regard has been used over a period of many centuries. But I would point out this fact: that until comparatively modern times the dominant Christian theological exegesis was one which connected the image of God in man with man's immortal soul, his reason, his spirituality; something of this is already present as early as the Apocryphal Wisdom of Solomon ii. 23. Under this sort of interpretation the relation of man to the rest of nature, and especially the animal world, tended to be thought of not as the practical question of control, technology and exploitation, but as the *superiority* of the rational being, with his immortal soul, over that which is soulless and mortal. As I have already suggested, it was only in fairly modern times, with a loss of conviction in the traditional exegesis (largely because historical study made it seem now quite unlikely that the Hebrew Genesis was concerned with rationality and the immortal soul) that an exegesis which laid great emphasis on the dominion of man over nature became prevalent. We must therefore doubt whether the Genesis passage, under the interpretation which it enjoyed for most of its historical life, can have had so great an effect in encouraging man in practical measures of exploitation and domination.

Moreover, the major Old Testament creation stories show little interest in the origins of technology. This is striking, because considerable elements of technological legend are quite common in stories of the beginnings of mankind. Something of the kind is no doubt mirrored in the idea of the successive ages, the Golden, Silver, Bronze and Iron. A particularly good example is furnished by the Phoenician legends transmitted to us by the Greek writer Philo of Byblos.[27] He said that he got his material from the Phoenician Sanchuniathon, who had lived about the time of the Trojan Wars—very roughly, in other words, about the time of the earliest Old Testament writings. This estimate may well be a wild one, but nevertheless the material seems to be well comparable with that of the Old Testament. This story—which in its present form may indeed be much distorted—combines the genre of theogony with that of what we may term technogony: it begins with genealogies and matings in the world of the gods but eventually comes down to a more human and practical level, telling of who first discovered food from trees, the making of fire by the rubbing of sticks, the making of rafts and boats, the use of animal skins for clothing, the working of iron, the making of brick walls, and so on.

It is easy to show that this kind of technological story of human origins existed in the biblical world, for a fragment of one is found in the tale of Cain and Abel, the similarity of which to Philo of Byblos has often been remarked.[28] This tale, though

27. Greek text in F. Jacoby, *Die Fragmente der griechischen Historiker,* Dritter Teil, C II, no. 790, pp. 802–24. For a useful discussion see F. Løkkegaard, "Some Comments on the Sanchuniathon Tradition," *Studia Theologica,* viii (1954), 51–76.
28. E.g. Skinner, *Genesis,* p. 123.

now set as sequel to the story of Adam and Eve, may in an earlier stage have been part of an independent story of human origins. Right at the start it notes the occupational difference between Cain and Abel, and later it goes on to tell a story of human discovery, saying who was the first to live in tents and keep cattle, the first to have musical instruments, and the first to use bronze and iron; also it tells who founded the first city. Thus the genre of the technologically-interested legend of origins is found in fragments in the Old Testament, and it certainly was well known in the environment; but in the central biblical stories of creation ana human origins it is scarcely represented at all. There is little interest in the development of tools and weapons; nothing of this kind figures in the depiction of the central personages like Abraham.[29] Nimrod the "mighty hunter," possibly also a fragment from an early technogony, is in the present Genesis characteristically a peripheral figure, lacking any real connection with the story. The prosperity of Isaac as a farmer is reported (Gen. xxvi. 12), but there is no interest in his agricultural methods; the matter belongs rather to the blessing of God which was upon him.

Something similar can be said about the depiction of God. For this purpose the Bible uses only to a limited extent images from the life of the craftsman and artisan. It forms a contrast with both the Near Eastern environment, in which artisan deities like the Ugaritic K-th-r w-Ḫ-s-s are well known, and the situation in Greece, where the conception of God as a great

29. There is an amusing contrast in a quaint story found in the *Book of Jubilees* (a sort of later rewriting of Genesis), xi. 23–24. In Ur of the Chaldees at sowing-time much trouble was caused by ravens, which devoured the seed, and Abraham (!) instructed the carpenters how to integrate a seed-box with the plough, so that the seed was immediately covered with earth and made safe from the ravens. This is a totally different atmosphere from that of Genesis.

designer and artificer was highly developed.

The place where the Old Testament takes an interest in technology is not within the creation stories and historical literature, but in the wisdom literature. Here, and notably in Job, quite a lot is said about the exploitation of the riches of the earth, the mining for precious stones, the possibilities of and the limits of exploration by land and sea. It is in Ecclesiastes, one of the later products of this literature, that we find a writer facing the problems for faith that arise when the world process, "all that happens under the sun," is contemplated. It is Solomon, the legendary patron of this strain in Israelite thought, who is credited (1 Kings v. 13; EV iv. 33) with discourse about trees, about animals and birds, reptiles and fishes. The fact that this sort of proto-scientific interest is cultivated in the wisdom current of literature, rather than elsewhere, is significant.[30] Of all the Old Testament material, it is this which expresses a realization of an international and even inter-religious culture. The sort of scientific and technological interests that it reveals are *not* explicitly derived from the specific revelation of God to Israel.

If in fact Hebrew culture contained unique insights, even *in nuce,* which were later to bear fruit in the form of science and technology, one would have expected at least some minimal distinctiveness in point of science and technology to have attached to the material life of ancient Israel.[31] I do not, however, know of any way at all in which such distinctiveness could be

30. The other place where we could locate a sort of proto-scientific interest in Israel would be outside of the canonical Old Testament, i.e. in the apocalyptic literature, with its astronomical speculations. Note the parallel with the passage from Jubilees cited above, p. 67, n. 29. For a stimulating recent study of apocalyptic thought in relation to modern theological problems, see K. Koch, *The Rediscovery of Apocalyptic* (London, 1972).

31. Cf. also Macquarrie, p. 5: "The Hebrews themselves held to a doctrine of creation for several centuries, but they developed no science worth mentioning."

argued, whether we look for our facts to archaeology or turn to the Bible's own account of the matter. The material and technical culture was, so far as I know, absolutely continuous with that of Israel's neighbours.[32] True, the position which we are discussing did not assert that science and technology were already present in biblical Israel, but only that biblical Israel formed the ideas upon which their later rise was dependent. Nevertheless it is striking if one has to admit that these ideas, which were to be so essential to scientific progress two millennia later, had absolutely no such effect in their own time. The fact that this was so militates, in spite of all possible qualification, against the hypothesis of an integral relation between biblical thought and the rise of science; and the same is true of the doctrine of creation in its developed Christian form.

What then are the intellectual antecedents of modern science? I would not consider myself competent to offer a scholarly opinion about such a complicated matter, but some sort of generalization must be ventured. Basically I would be against all attempts to explain a complicated modern process by setting it against two or three simple and remote models such as "biblical thought" or "Greek thought." I would see the rise of science in the image of a "take-off," where the most relevant forces and pressures are not the ones at the beginning of the process but those nearer the critical point; the important decisions then would be those made from the latter part of the Middle Ages onward.[33] But if it were insisted that one must specify the ana-

32. The building which most interested the biblical Israelites, i.e. the Solomonic temple, was expressly of Phoenician craftsmanship. The story is interested in its patterns and dimensions because of the religious significance of the entire building; such interest as there is in the methods of construction used is entirely religiously, and not at all technologically, motivated.

33. It is interesting that the strong points of Lynn White's original article lie in the Middle Ages, which are his own special period. In the same regard, he

logue of science in remote antiquity and the source from which it has developed, I personally do not doubt that the basic intellectual ancestry of modern science must be found in Greek science. In spite of the enormous differences between Greek science and modern science, and in spite of the revolution against Greek science through which modern science came to birth, it seems to me that there is an undeniable continuity on the level of history of ideas. Important concepts and aspects of method are carried over, and essential social characteristics, such as a widely enquiring spirit and a freedom of thought and discussion, are held in common.

As I have already said, this does not mean that there is no connection between the Jewish-Christian doctrine of creation and the rise of science. The crisis of Greek science and the rise of modern science were intricately linked with the crisis of medieval religion and the birth of Protestantism and modern liberalism and humanism. Such things as openness to new ideas, and freedom for research and criticism of tradition, which are essential to the health of science, were in the history of thought deeply connected with the religious development. It does not follow from this that in terms of *content* the religious tradition furnished essential presuppositions for science. The argument that many early scientists were clergymen or were devoted students of the Bible and theology seems to me to be nugatory. This was true of the educated man in general in those times. Moreover, the ideas then entertained about a subject like the Old Testament view of reality were worlds apart from the concep-

---

rightly observes that the area in which modern science arose is not coterminous with Christendom. Modern science, he rightly sees, belongs to the West, and many centuries of Christianity in the Greek East did not generate it there. But does this not only lead to the conclusion that the decisive factors in the rise or non-rise of science are something other than the presence or absence of the Jewish-Christian doctrine of creation?

tions of modern scholarship; and the linkage alleged between Hebrew thought and science is something that depends entirely on a modern, and not on the traditional, view of the interests and perceptions of the Old Testament.

The interpretation of the Old Testament in this whole matter depends to a high degree not on what it itself says but upon what is imagined to be in contrast with it. As I said at the beginning of this lecture, it is commonly held that in other religions than the biblical, nature was understood to be in some way divine. Hebrew faith uniquely broke through this barrier and enabled men to see nature for what it is. According to some accounts, the history-centered character of Hebrew faith enabled it to escape from bondage to nature.[34] Because this picture of the ancient religions provides the background to the Old Testament and delineates the opposition against which books like Genesis are supposed to have been written, it becomes decisive in interpretation. But can this picture of a world of nature-religions be valid? Does the evidence from ancient texts support it? The picture of the ancient religions, against which the Hebrew contribution has been set, seems to depend excessively on purely theological and philosophical analysis of what it *must* have been like, too little on expert historical analysis of what it *was* like.[35] Unquestionably aspects of the ancient religions (or of some of

34. See Cox, op. cit. pp. 22 f.; "God in Nature and History," pp. 9 f. Note in the latter, p. 9, the statement that "For the primitive and ancient religions of the Middle East, God or the gods are mainly revealed in nature. Nature is the external aspect of divine reality." But do we know that this is so? Cf. also the schematic assertion, ibid., p. 10: "In the ancient religions, history is naturalized; in Israel nature is historicized." Contrast with this B. Albrektson, *History and the Gods* (Lund, 1967).

35. In this much must depend on the discussions of specialists, such as Assyriologists, on the function of myths within ancient cultures. A key position is held, for instance, by the ideas of Th. Jacobsen. On this see G. S. Kirk, *Myth: Its Meaning and Functions in Ancient and Other Cultures* (Cambridge, 1970), especially pp. 84–118. W. G. Lambert, in his *Babylonian Wisdom Literature*, pp. 1–20, suggests that already in Akkadian myths the gods have ceased to be aspects of nature; see Kirk, op. cit. pp. 119 f.

them—in this they differ from one another) can be understood as suggesting that divinity was in nature or that nature was in harmony with the divine. But it seems to me very hard to interpret all the variety of the mythological texts as if they in fact added up to a declaration of harmony between nature and the divine. Still less can I understand it when the very same characterization is applied to Greek science; and Foster's generally careful philosophical analysis in the articles mentioned seems to be complemented by a much wilder sort of generalization when he writes that the attitude of the Greek scientists was "an intellectualized form of nature worship," a statement cited with apparent approval by Baillie.[36] Whatever seems to be theoretically likely or probable, hard evidence does not seem to have been produced to show what sort of connection there was between nature elements in ancient mythologies on the one hand and the way in which the ancient peoples in practice perceived nature. In particular, it is not clear that cultures which had advanced nature-religions or advanced mythologies were thereby necessarily inhibited from making remarkable technological advances. The ancient Egyptians, in whose religion the animal realm was particularly closely associated with the divine, were able to advance to the building of the pyramids in a very brief space of time. If some of the pictures of ancient religion which have been painted are accurate, I do not see how the pyramids could have been built.[37] The illustration is not an idle

36. Baillie, p. 31; I have not seen the original source. Foster's definition of paganism as "the failure to distinguish God from nature" seems to me schematic and dogmatic and poorly related to the facts of ancient religion (*Mind,* xliv. 442); and cf. his assertion that "the identification of God with Nature finds its earliest expression in the deification of natural powers which is characteristic of the Greek polytheistic religion" (*Mind,* xliii. 456).
37. This objection could be advanced for instance against the argument of Berdyaev, cited by Baillie, p. 30, to the effect that so long as man was in

one, for the experiences of technology in the form of mining and similar activities as mentioned in the Old Testament most probably go back to Egyptian initiatives.

We return then to the modern ecological controversy from which we began. If my arguments are correct, there is much less direct connection between biblical faith and modern science than has been recently believed in some theological currents. The Jewish-Christian doctrine of creation is therefore much less responsible for the ecological crisis than is suggested by arguments such as those of Lynn White. On the contrary, the biblical foundations of that doctrine would tend in the opposite direction, away from a licence to exploit and towards a duty to respect and to protect. I do not say this out of a wish to avoid responsibility for what has been done wrongly; but if one is to speak of responsibility, one has the duty to see that it is fairly adjudged. My original interest in this subject was not kindled by the present ecological discussion, but rather by my own doubts about the theological argument which linked the Bible to the rise of modern science. This argument needs to be entirely rethought for the sake of truth, whatever its relation to the ecological controversy. But, as far as one must speak of responsibility and guilt, I would say that the great modern exploitation of nature has taken place under the reign of a liberal humanism in which man no longer conceives of himself as being under a creator, and in which therefore his place of dominance in the universe and his right to dispose of nature for his own ends is, unlike the situation in the Bible, unlimited.

This leads me in conclusion to mention certain insights of the Bible which are likely to be relevant to our present situation. I

communion with nature and based his life upon mythology, he could not have built railways or invented the telephone.

do not justify these by building a chain in the history of ideas between the Bible and modern science, nor do I expect to wring from the Bible answers to questions of which the writers were entirely unaware; I merely point to them as things that are relevant.

Firstly, I would remind you of the insistence of the Genesis creation story that all that was created was good. This point is strongly emphasized, and seems to have a considerable distinctiveness about it. I would have thought that a conviction of the goodness of the created world would be a powerful motive for all sorts of action to control and limit the exploitation and pollution of it.

Secondly, the world of the Genesis creation story is an ordered world. The story is built upon a process of separation and ordering; it is interested in different levels of created being, in different functions and different species. I do not suggest that the scientific principle of order derived from Genesis; but there is something here in common between the two, and it is something which enables the reader of the Bible to view with a sense of community the researches of science, the achievements of technological control, and the work of the accompanying social planning.

Thirdly, the whole framework of Genesis i is intended to suggest that man is man when he is in his place within nature. His dominion over nature is given little definition; but, in general, its content is less exploitation and more leadership, a sort of primary liturgical place. That man's dominion or eminence should from now on increasingly be applied to the task of conserving and caring for the natural resources of God's world, by using man's own scientific, technical and planning powers to limit and control what these same powers, if left unlimited, would perpetrate, is entirely consonant with the tendency of the Old Testament.

Fourthly, such insights on incipient science and technology as the Old Testament offered lie primarily in the Wisdom literature. The activities described are something in which the biblical men delight, something which they respect and admire; they recognize that they are a part of God's world, a part which extends out into far vistas of mystery which the men of that time could not penetrate. They recognized that world of techniques, but they also did not try to claim it for their own; it was international and extended beyond Israel. They could associate with it, freely and happily; they did not feel constrained to justify it by deriving it from their own inner religious tradition, or to magnify their own religious tradition by representing it as the source of these insights. Is not this something of a good example for the Jewish-Christian idea of creation, as it associates itself with the world of science in our own time?

The Cultural Basis for Our Environmental Crisis

LEWIS W. MONCRIEF

One hundred years ago at almost any location in the United States, potable water was no farther away than the closest brook or stream. Today there are hardly any streams in the United States, except in a few high mountainous reaches, that can safely satisfy human thirst without chemical treatment. An oft-mentioned satisfaction in the lives of urbanites in an earlier era was a leisurely stroll in late afternoon to get a breath of fresh air in a neighborhood park or along a quiet street. Today in many of our major metropolitan areas it is difficult to find a quiet, peaceful place to take a leisurely stroll and sometimes impossible to get a breath of fresh air. These contrasts point up the dramatic changes that have occurred in the quality of our environment.

It is not my intent in this article, however, to document the existence of an environmental crisis but rather to discuss the cultural basis for such a crisis. Particular attention will be given to the institutional structures as expressions of our culture.

SOURCE: *Science*, 170 (30 October 1970), 508–512. This article is based on an address given at a "Man and Environment" Conference at Arizona State University on 16 April 1970.

SOCIAL ORGANIZATION

In her book entitled *Social Institutions*[1] J. O. Hertzler classified all social institutions into nine functional categories: (i) economic and industrial, (ii) matrimonial and domestic, (iii) political, (iv) religious, (v) ethical, (vi) educational, (vii) communications, (viii) esthetic, and (ix) health. Institutions exist to carry on each of these functions in all cultures, regardless of their location or relative complexity. Thus, it is not surprising that one of the analytical criteria used by anthropologists in the study of various cultures is the comparison and contrast of the various social institutions as to form and relative importance.[2]

A number of attempts have been made to explain attitudes and behavior that are commonly associated with one institutional function as the result of influence from a presumably independent institutional factor. The classic example of such an analysis is *The Protestant Ethic and the Spirit of Capitalism* by Max Weber.[3] In this significant work Weber attributes much of the economic and industrial growth in Western Europe and North America to capitalism, which, he argued, was an economic form that developed as a result of the religious teachings of Calvin, particularly spiritual determinism.

Social scientists have been particularly active in attempting to assess the influence of religious teaching and practice and of economic motivation on other institutional forms and behavior and on each other. In this connection, L. White[4] suggested that

1. J. O. Hertzler, *Social Institutions* (McGraw-Hill, New York, 1929), pp. 47–64.
2. L. A. White, *The Science of Culture* (Farrar, Straus & Young, New York, 1949), pp. 121–145.
3. M. Weber, *The Protestant Ethic and the Spirit of Capitalism*, translated by T. Parsons (Scribner's, New York, 1958).
4. L. White, Jr., *Science* **155**, 1203 (1967).

the exploitative attitude that has prompted much of the environmental crisis in Western Europe and North America is a result of the teachings of the Judeo-Christian tradition, which conceives of man as superior to all other creation and of everything else as created for his use and enjoyment. He goes on to contend that the only way to reduce the ecologic crisis which we are now facing is to "reject the Christian axiom that nature has no reason for existence save to serve man." As with other ideas that appear to be new and novel, Professor White's observations have begun to be widely circulated and accepted in scholarly circles, as witness the article by religious writer E. B. Fiske in the *New York Times* earlier this year.[5] In this article, note is taken of the fact that several prominent theologians and theological groups have accepted this basic premise that Judeo-Christian doctrine regarding man's relation to the rest of creation is at the root of the West's environmental crisis. I would suggest that the wide acceptance of such a simplistic explanation is at this point based more on fad than on fact.

Certainly, no fault can be found with White's statement that "Human ecology is deeply conditioned by beliefs about our nature and destiny—that is, by religion." However, to argue that it is the primary conditioner of human behavior toward the environment is much more than the data that he cites to support this proposition will bear. For example, White himself notes very early in his article that there is evidence for the idea that man has been dramatically altering his environment since antiquity. If this be true, and there is evidence that it is, then this mediates against the idea that the Judeo-Christian religion uniquely predisposes cultures within which it thrives to exploit

5. E. B. Fiske, "The link between faith and ecology," *New York Times* (4 January 1970), section 4, p. 5.

their natural resources with indiscretion. White's own examples weaken his argument considerably. He points out that human intervention in the periodic flooding of the Nile River basin and the fire-drive method of hunting by prehistoric man have both probably wrought significant "unnatural" changes in man's environment. The absence of Judeo-Christian influence in these cases is obvious.

It seems tenable to affirm that the role played by religion in man-to-man and man-to-environment relationships is one of establishing a very broad system of allowable beliefs and behavior and of articulating and invoking a system of social and spiritual rewards for those who conform and of negative sanctions for individuals or groups who approach or cross the pale of the religiously unacceptable. In other words, it defines the ball park in which the game is played, and, by the very nature of the park, some types of games cannot be played. However, the kind of game that ultimately evolves is not itself defined by the ball park. For example, where animism is practiced, it is not likely that the believers will indiscriminately destroy objects of nature because such activity would incur the danger of spiritual and social sanctions. However, the fact that another culture does not associate spiritual beings with natural objects does not mean that such a culture will invariably ruthlessly exploit its resources. It simply means that there are fewer social and psychological constraints against such action.

In the remainder of this article, I present an alternative set of hypotheses based on cultural variables which, it seems to me, are more plausible and more defensible as an explanation of the environmental crisis that is now confronting us.

No culture has been able to completely screen out the egocentric tendencies of human beings. There also exists in all cultures a status hierarchy of positions and values, with certain groups partially or totally excluded from access to these normatively desirable goals. Historically, the differences in most cultures between the "rich" and the "poor" have been great. The many very poor have often produced the wealth for the few who controlled the means of production. There may have been no alternative where scarcity of supply and unsatiated demand were economic reality. Still, the desire for a "better life" is universal; that is, the desire for higher status positions and the achievement of culturally defined desirable goals is common to all societies.

THE EXPERIENCE IN THE WESTERN WORLD

In the West two significant revolutions that occurred in the 18th and 19th centuries completely redirected its political, social, and economic destiny.[6] These two types of revolutions were unique to the West until very recently. The French revolution marked the beginnings of widespread democratization. In specific terms, this revolution involved a redistribution of the means of production and a reallocation of the natural and human resources that are an integral part of the production process. In effect new channels of social mobility were created, which theoretically made more wealth accessible to more people. Even though the revolution was partially perpetrated in the guise of overthrowing the control of presumably Christian institutions and of destroying the influence of God over the minds of men, still it would be superficial to argue that Christianity did not influence

6. R. A. Nisbet, *The Sociological Tradition* (Basic Books, New York, 1966), pp. 21–44. Nisbet gives here a perceptive discourse on the social and political implications of the democratic and industrial revolutions to the Western world.

this revolution. After all, biblical teaching is one of the strongest of all pronouncements concerning human dignity and individual worth.

At about the same time but over a more extended period, another kind of revolution was taking place, primarily in England. As White points out very well, this phenomenon, which began with a number of technological innovations, eventually consummated a marriage with natural science and began to take on the character that it has retained until today.[7] With this revolution the productive capacity of each worker was amplified by several times his potential prior to the revolution. It also became feasible to produce goods that were not previously producible on a commercial scale.

Later, with the integration of the democratic and the technological ideals, the increased wealth began to be distributed more equitably among the population. In addition, as the capital to land ratio increased in the production process and the demand grew for labor to work in the factories, large populations from the agrarian hinterlands began to concentrate in the emerging industrial cities. The stage was set for the development of the conditions that now exist in the Western world.

With growing affluence for an increasingly large segment of the population, there generally develops an increased demand for goods and services. The usual by-product of this affluence is

7. It should be noted that a slower and less dramatic process of democratization was evident in English history at a much earlier date than the French revolution. Thus, the concept of democracy was probably a much more pervasive influence in English than in French life. However, a rich body of philosophic literature regarding the rationale for democracy resulted from the French revolution. Its counterpart in English literature is much less conspicuous. It is an interesting aside to suggest that perhaps the industrial revolution would not have been possible except for the more broad-based ownership of the means of production that resulted from the long-standing process of democratization in England.

waste from both the production and consumption processes. The disposal of that waste is further complicated by the high concentration of heavy waste producers in urban areas. Under these conditions the maxim that "Dilution is the solution to pollution" does not withstand the test of time, because the volume of such wastes is greater than the system can absorb and purify through natural means. With increasing population, increasing production, increasing urban concentrations, and increasing real median incomes for well over a hundred years, it is not surprising that our environment has taken a terrible beating in absorbing our filth and refuse.

THE AMERICAN SITUATION

The North American colonies of England and France were quick to pick up the technical and social innovations that were taking place in their motherlands. Thus, it is not surprising that the inclination to develop an industrial and manufacturing base is observable rather early in the colonies. A strong trend toward democratization also evidenced itself very early in the struggle for nationhood. In fact, Thistlewaite notes the significance of the concept of democracy as embodied in French thought to the framers of constitutional government in the colonies.[8]

From the time of the dissolution of the Roman Empire, resource ownership in the Western world was vested primarily with the monarchy or the Roman Catholic Church, which in turn bestowed control of the land resources on vassals who pledged fealty to the sovereign. Very slowly the concept of private ownership developed during the Middle Ages in Europe, until it finally developed into the fee simple concept.

8. F. Thistlewaite, *The Great Experiment* (Cambridge Univ. Press, London, 1955), pp. 33–34, 60.

In America, however, national policy from the outset was designed to convey ownership of the land and other natural resources into the hands of the citizenry. Thomas Jefferson was perhaps more influential in crystallizing this philosophy in the new nation than anyone else. It was his conviction that an agrarian society made up of small landowners would furnish the most stable foundation for building the nation.[9] This concept has received support up to the present and, against growing economic pressures in recent years, through government programs that have encouraged the conventional family farm. This point is clearly relevant to the subject of this article because it explains how the natural resources of the nation came to be controlled not by a few aristocrats but by many citizens. It explains how decisions that ultimately degrade the environment are made not only by corporation boards and city engineers but by millions of owners of our natural resources. This is democracy exemplified!

CHALLENGE OF THE FRONTIER

Perhaps the most significant interpretation of American history has been Fredrick Jackson Turner's much criticized thesis that the western frontier was the prime force in shaping our society.[10] In his own words,

> *If one would understand why we are today one nation, rather than a collection of isolated states, he must study this economic and social consolidation of the country. . . . The effect of the Indian frontier as a consolidating agent in our history is important.*

9. Ibid, pp. 59–68.
10. F. J. Turner, *The Frontier in American History* (Henry Holt, New York, 1920 and 1947).

He further postulated that the nation experienced a series of frontier challenges that moved across the continent in waves. These included the explorers' and traders' frontier, the Indian frontier, the cattle frontier, and three distinct agrarian frontiers. His thesis can be extended to interpret the expansionist period of our history in Panama, in Cuba, and in the Philippines as a need for a continued frontier challenge.

Turner's insights furnish a starting point for suggesting a second variable in analyzing the cultural basis of the United States' environmental crisis. As the nation began to expand westward, the settlers faced many obstacles, including a primitive transportation system, hostile Indians, and the absence of physical and social security. To many frontiersmen, particularly small farmers, many of the natural resources that are now highly valued were originally perceived more as obstacles than as assets. Forests needed to be cleared to permit farming. Marshes needed to be drained. Rivers needed to be controlled. Wildlife often represented a competitive threat in addition to being a source of food. Sod was considered a nuisance—to be burned, plowed, or otherwise destroyed to permit "desirable" use of the land.

Undoubtedly, part of this attitude was the product of perceiving these resources as inexhaustible. After all, if a section of timber was put to the torch to clear it for farming, it made little difference because there was still plenty to be had very easily. It is no coincidence that the "First Conservation Movement" began to develop about 1890. At that point settlement of the frontier was almost complete. With the passing of the frontier era of American history, it began to dawn on people that our resources were indeed exhaustible. This realization ushered in a new philosophy of our national government toward natural resources management under the guidance of Theodore Roosevelt and Gifford Pinchot. Samuel Hays[11] has characterized this movement as the appearance of a new "Gospel of Efficiency" in the management and utilization of our natural resources.

THE PRESENT AMERICAN SCENE

America is the archetype of what happens when democracy, technology, urbanization, capitalistic mission, and antagonism (or apathy) toward natural environment are blended together. The present situation is characterized by three dominant features that mediate against quick solution to this impending crisis: (i) an absence of personal moral direction concerning our treatment of our natural resources, (ii) an inability on the part of our social institutions to make adjustments to this stress, and (iii) an abiding faith in technology.

The first characteristic is the absence of personal moral direction. There is moral disparity when a corporation executive can receive a prison sentence for embezzlement but be congratulated for increasing profits by ignoring pollution abatement laws. That the absolute cost to society of the second act may be infinitely greater than the first is often not even considered.

The moral principle that we are to treat others as we would want to be treated seems as appropriate a guide as it ever has been. The rarity of such teaching and the even more uncommon instance of its being practiced help to explain how one municipality can, without scruple, dump its effluent into a stream even though it may do irreparable damage to the resource and add tremendously to the cost incurred by downstream municipalities that use the same water. Such attitudes are not restricted to

11. S. P. Hays, *Conservation and the Gospel of Efficiency* (Harvard Univ. Press, Cambridge, Mass., 1959).

any one culture. There appears to be an almost universal tendency to maximize self-interests and a widespread willingness to shift production costs to society to promote individual ends.

Undoubtedly, much of this behavior is the result of ignorance. If our accounting systems were more efficient in computing the cost of such irresponsibility both to the present generation and to those who will inherit the environment we are creating, steps would undoubtedly be taken to enforce compliance with measures designed to conserve resources and protect the environment. And perhaps if the total costs were known, we might optimistically speculate that more voluntary compliance would result.

A second characteristic of our current situation involves institutional inadequacies. It has been said that "what belongs to everyone belongs to no one." This maxim seems particularly appropriate to the problem we are discussing. So much of our environment is so apparently abundant that it is considered a free commodity. Air and water are particularly good examples. Great liberties have been permitted in the use and abuse of these resources for at least two reasons. First, these resources have typically been considered of less economic value than other natural resources except when conditions of extreme scarcity impose limiting factors. Second, the right of use is more difficult to establish for resources that are not associated with a fixed location.

Government, as the institution representing the corporate interests of all its citizens, has responded to date with dozens of legislative acts and numerous court decisions which give it authority to regulate the use of natural resources. However, the decisiveness to act has thus far been generally lacking. This indecisiveness cannot be understood without noting that the simplistic models that depict the conflict as that of a few powerful special interests versus "The People" are altogether inadequate. A very large proportion of the total citizenry is implicated in environmental degradation; the responsibility ranges from that of the board and executives of a utility company who might wish to thermally pollute a river with impunity to that of the average citizen who votes against a bond issue to improve the efficiency of a municipal sanitation system in order to keep his taxes from being raised. The magnitude of irresponsibility among individuals and institutions might be characterized as falling along a continuum from highly irresponsible to indirectly responsible. With such a broad base of interests being threatened with every change in resource policy direction, it is not surprising, although regrettable, that government has been so indecisive.

A third characteristic of the present American scene is an abiding faith in technology. It is very evident that the idea that technology can overcome almost any problem is widespread in Western society. This optimism exists in the face of strong evidence that much of man's technology, when misused, has produced harmful results, particularly in the long run. The reasoning goes something like this: "After all, we have gone to the moon. All we need to do is allocate enough money and brainpower and we can solve any problem."

It is both interesting and alarming that many people view technology almost as something beyond human control. Rickover put it this way:[12]

It troubles me that we are so easily pressured by purveyors of technology into permitting so-called "progress" to alter our lives without attempting

12. H. G. Rickover, *Amer. Forests* **75,** 13 (August 1969).

to control it—as if technology were an irrepressible force of nature to which we must meekly submit.

He goes on to add:

It is important to maintain a humanistic attitude toward technology; to recognize clearly that since it is the product of human effort, technology can have no legitimate purpose but to serve man—man in general, not merely some men; future generations, not merely those who currently wish to gain advantage for themselves; man in the totality of his humanity, encompassing all his manifold interests and needs, not merely some one particular concern of his. When viewed humanistically, technology is seen not as an end in itself but a means to an end, the end being determined by man himself in accordance with the laws prevailing in his society.

In short, it is one thing to appreciate the value of technology; it is something else entirely to view it as our environmental savior—which will save us in spite of ourselves.

CONCLUSION

The forces of democracy, technology, urbanization, increasing individual wealth, and an aggressive attitude toward nature seem to be directly related to the environmental crisis now being confronted in the Western world. The Judeo-Christian tradition has probably influenced the character of each of these forces. However, to isolate religious tradition as a cultural component and to contend that it is the "historical root of our ecologic crisis" is a bold affirmation for which there is little historical or scientific support.

To assert that the primary cultural condition that has created our environmental crisis is Judeo-Christian teaching avoids several hard questions. For example: Is there less tendency for those who control the resources in non-Christian cultures to live in extravagant affluence with attendant high levels of waste and inefficient consumption? If non-Judeo-Christian cultures had the same levels of economic productivity, urbanization, and high average household incomes, is there evidence to indicate that these cultures would not exploit or disregard nature as our culture does?

If our environmental crisis is a "religious problem," why are other parts of the world experiencing in various degrees the same environmental problems that we are so well acquainted with in the Western world? It is readily observable that the science and technology that developed on a large scale first in the West have been adopted elsewhere. Judeo-Christian tradition has not been adopted as a predecessor to science and technology on a comparable scale. Thus, all White can defensibly argue is that the West developed modern science and technology *first.* This says nothing about the origin or existence of a particular ethic toward our environment.

In essence, White has proposed this simple model:

I	II	III
JUDEO-CHRISTIAN TRADITION	SCIENCE AND TECHNOLOGY	ENVIRONMENTAL DEGRADATION

I have suggested here that, at best, Judeo-Christian teaching has had only an indirect effect on the treatment of our environment. The model could be characterized as follows:

I	II	III	IV
JUDEO-CHRISTIAN TRADITION	1) CAPITALISM (WITH THE ATTENDANT DEVELOPMENT OF SCIENCE AND TECHNOLOGY) 2) DEMOCRATIZATION	1) URBANIZATION 2) INCREASED WEALTH 3) INCREASED POPULATION 4) INDIVIDUAL RESOURCE OWNERSHIP	ENVIRONMENTAL DEGRADATION

Even here, the link between Judeo-Christian tradition and the proposed dependent variables certainly has the least empirical support. One need only look at the veritable mountain of Weber's conclusions in *The Protestant Ethic and the Spirit of Capitalism* to sense the tenuous nature of this link. The second and third phases of this model are common to many parts of the world. Phase I is not.

Jean Mayer,[13] the eminent food scientist, gave an appropriate conclusion about the cultural basis for our environmental crisis:

It might be bad in China with 700 million poor people but 700 million rich Chinese would wreck China in no time. . . . It's the rich who wreck the environment . . . occupy much more space, consume more of each natural resource, disturb ecology more, litter the landscape . . . and create more pollution.

13. J. Mayer and T G. Harris, *Psychol. Today* **3,** 46 and 48 (January 1970).

Discrepancies between Environmental Attitude and Behaviour: Examples from Europe and China

YI-FU TUAN

Discrepancy between stated ideal and reality is a worrisome fact of our daily experience: in the political field one learns to discriminate between an orator's fulsome profession and what he can or will, in fact, carry out. The history of environmental ideas, however, has been pursued as an academic discipline largely in detachment from the question of how—if at all—these ideas guide the course of action, or how they arise out of it. Needless to say, there are many paradigmatic views of nature, such as those of science, that have great explicatory power and may, once they are applied, affect the lives of many people; but in themselves they do not enjoin a specific course of action. In contrast, the acceptance of certain specific environmental ideas can have a definite effect on decision and on behaviour. If it is widely held, for example, that a dry and sunny climate is a great restorer of health, we may suppose that an appreciable number

SOURCE: *The Canadian Geographer,* 12, no. 3 (1968), 176–191. Reprinted by permission of the author. The illustrations originally accompanying this article have been omitted.

of people will seek out these areas for health. But what of less specific ideas? We may believe that a world-view which puts nature in subservience to man will lead to the exploitation of nature by man; and one that regards man as simply a component in nature will entail a modest view of his rights and capabilities, and so lead to the establishment of a harmonious relationship between man and his natural environment. But is this correct? And if essentially correct, how direct or tenuous is the link? These are some of the questions I wish to explore with the help of examples from Europe and China. The discrepancies are noted here; their resolution must await another occasion.

I

To the question, what is a fundamental difference between the European and the Chinese attitude towards nature, most people with any opinion at all will probably make some such reply: that the European sees nature as subordinate to him whereas the Chinese sees himself as a part of nature. Taken as a broad generalization and with a grain of salt there is much truth in this distinction; a truth illustrated with diagrammatic force when one compares the formal European garden of the seventeenth century with the Chinese naturalistic garden. The geometric contrast reflects fundamental differences in environmental evaluation. The formal European garden in the style of the Le Nôtre was designed to produce a limited number of imposing prospects. It can be appreciated to the full only at a limited number of favoured spots where the onlooker is invited by the garden's design to gaze at distant vistas. Or, seen in another way, the European garden is a grandiose setting for man; in deference to him, nature is straitjacketed in court dress. The Chinese garden, on the other hand, is designed to produce almost constantly shifting scenes: there are no set prospects. The nature of the garden requires the perceiver to move along a winding path and to be more than visually involved with the landscape. It is not nature that is required to put on court dress in deference to man: rather, it is man who must lay aside his formalistic pretensions in order to enter nature.

This widely recognized distinction is valid and important. On the other hand, by the crude test of the total tonnage of earth removed there may not be so very much difference between the European formal and the Chinese naturalistic garden. Both are human artifacts. It is not widely known that some of the famous scenic areas of China are works of man rather than of geologic processes. The West Lake of Hang-chou, for example, was celebrated by T'ang and Sung poets and it remains to this day an adornment of China. To the casual visitor, the West Lake region may appear to be a striking illustration of how the works of man can blend modestly into the magistral context of nature. However, the pervasiveness of nature is largely an illusion induced by art. Some of the islands in the lake are man-made. Moreover, the lake itself is artificial and has to be maintained with care. In the thirteenth century, military patrols, under the command of specially appointed officials, looked after its policing and maintenance; it was forbidden, for example, to throw any rubbish into it or to plant in it lotuses or water-chestnuts. Peasants were recruited to clear and enlarge the lake, to keep it from being cluttered up by vegetation and silt.[1] Hang-chou's environs, then, owe much of their calm, harmonious beauty to human art and effort. The sense of open nature in Hang-chou is enhanced by

1. Gernet, Jacques, *Daily Life in China on the Eve of the Mongol Invasion 1250–1276* (London, 1962), pp. 51–52.

its scale: the West Lake region is a cluster of public and semi-public parks. In the much smaller compass of the private garden the illusion of pervasive nature is far more difficult to achieve: nevertheless the aim of the Chinese gardener was to achieve it with cleverly placed, water-worn limestone whose jagged outlines denoted wildness, and by means of winding footpaths that give the stroller an illusion of depth and space. In this line the Oriental's ultimate triumph is symbolized by the miniature garden, where wild nature is reduced to the scale of a dwarf landscape that can be fitted into a bowl. Complete artifice reigns: in the narrow confines of a bowl, shrubs are tortured by human skill into imitating the shape and posture of pines, the limbs of which may have been deformed by winds that swept the China Seas.

II

I have begun with a contrast and then proceeded to suggest that, from another perspective, the contrast is blurred. The publicized environmental ethos of a culture seldom covers more than a fraction of the total range of environmental behaviour. It is misleading to derive the one from the other. Simplifications that can mislead have at times been made. For example, Professor Lynn White has recently said: "What people do about their ecology depends on what they think about themselves in relation to things around them. Human ecology is deeply conditioned by beliefs about our nature and destiny—that is, by religion."[2] He goes on to say that the victory of Christianity over paganism was the greatest psychic revolution in Western cul-

2. White, Lynn, "The Historical Roots of Our Ecologic Crisis," *Science,* CLV (1967), 1205.

ture. In his view, despite all the talk of "the post-Christian age" and despite evident changes in the forms of modern thinking, the substance often remains amazingly akin to that of the Christian past. The Western man's daily habits of action are dominated by an implicit faith in perpetual progress which was unknown either to Greco-Roman antiquity or to the Orient. It is rooted in, and is indefensible apart from, Judeo-Christian teleology. Peoples of the Western world continue to live, as they have lived for about 1700 years, very largely in a context of Christian beliefs. And what has Christianity told people about their relations with the environment? Essentially that man, as something made in God's image, is not simply a part of nature; that God has planned the universe for man's benefit and rule. According to White, Christianity is the most anthropocentric religion the world has seen. It has not only established a dualism of man and nature but has also insisted that it is God's will that man exploit nature for his proper ends.[3]

To press the theme further, it is said that Christianity has destroyed antiquity's feeling for the holiness of landscapes and of natural things. The Greek religious tradition regarded the land not as an object to be exploited, or even as a visually pleasing setting, but as a true force which physically embodied the powers that ruled the world. Vincent Scully, the architectural historian, has argued that not only were certain landscapes regarded by the ancient Greeks as holy and expressive of specific gods, but also that the temples and the subsidiary buildings of their sanctuaries were so formed in themselves and so placed in the landscapes and to each other as to enhance, develop, and complement the basic meaning of the landscape.[4]

3. *Ibid.*
4. Scully, Vincent, *The Earth, The Temple, and The Gods* (New Haven, 1962), p. 3.

Martin Heidegger, a modern philosopher whose insights have been greatly influenced by early Greek philosophy, characterized the Greek temple as disclosing the earth on which it stands. The whiteness of the temple discloses the darkness and the strength of the rock underneath; it reveals the height and blueness of the sky, the power of the storm and the vastness of the sea.[5] In the Christian tradition, on the other hand, holiness was invested not in landscapes but in man-made altars, shrines, churches, and basilicas that dominated the landscapes. Constantine and Helen are said to have built basilicas over caves in the Holy Land to celebrate the triumph of Christianity over the "cave cultus" of the pagan world. In the Christian view it was not emanation from the earth but ritual that consecrated the site; man not nature bore the image of God and man's work, the hallowed edifice, symbolized the Christian cosmos. In pagan antiquity, at the level of the common people, each facet of nature had its own guardian spirit. Before one ventured to cut a tree, mine a mountain, or dam a brook, it was important to placate the spirit in charge of that particular situation, and to keep it placated. By destroying animistic beliefs, Christianity made it possible to exploit nature in a mood of indifference to the feeling of natural objects.

Much of this is now Western folklore and Lynn White is among the more recent writers to give it eloquent expression. The thesis, then, is that Christianity has introduced a fundamentally new way of evaluating the environment, and that this new evaluation has strongly affected Western man's traffic with the natural objects around him. The generalization is very useful, although one should take note of facts that appear to contradict

5. Vycinas, Vincent, *Earth and Gods: An Introduction to the Philosophy of Martin Heidegger* (The Hague, 1961), p. 13.

it. As Clarence Glàcken has demonstrated, in the ancient world there was no lack of interest in natural resources and their quick exploitation. Economic activities such as mining, the various ways of obtaining food, canal building, and drainage are clear proof of man's incessant restlessness in changing the earth about him.[6] Glacken points out that in Sophocles' *Antigone* there are lines which remind one of the eulogies of science in the eighteenth century, and of contemporary enthusiasm for man's control over nature. At one point in the play the chorus declares how the earth has felt man's ungentle touch:

> Oh, Earth is patient, and Earth is old,
> And a mother of Gods, but he breaketh her,
> To-ing, froing, with the plough teams going,
> Tearing the soil of her, year by year.[7]

The tearing of soil has led to erosion. In Plato's *Critias* there is the well-known passage in which he describes how the soils of Attica have been washed down to the sea. "And, just as happens in small islands, what now remains compared with what then existed is like the skeleton of a rich man, all the fat and soft earth have wasted away, and only the bare framework of the land being left." Plato then describes the former arable hills, fertile valleys, and forested mountains "of which there are visible signs even to this day." Mountains which today have food only for bees could, not so long ago, grow trees fit for the largest buildings. Cultivated trees provided pasturage for flocks, and the soil was well watered and the rain was "not lost to it,

6. Glacken, Clarence, *Traces on the Rhodian Shore* (Berkeley and Los Angeles, 1967), p. 118.
7. Sophocles, *Antigone,* transl. by Gilbert Murray in Arnold Toynbee, *Greek Historical Thought* (New York, 1952), p. 128.

as now, by flowing from the bare land to the sea."[8] Plato's comments sound remarkably modern; they remind us almost of the lamentations of latter-day conservationists.

If there is evidence of man's awareness of his power to transform nature—even destructively—in the time of Sophocles and Plato, there is evidence of much greater awareness of the almost limitless capabilities of man in Hellenistic times. Agriculture and related occupations such as cattle-breeding were then the most important source of wealth in the ancient world. Land reclamation was not a haphazard affair but one based on the science of mechanics and on practical experience with canal-digging, irrigation, and swamp drainage. It was a time of faith in progress. But far more than the Greeks, the Romans have imposed their will on the natural environment. And perhaps the most dramatic example of the triumph of the human will over the irregular lineaments of nature is the Roman grid method of dividing up the land. As Bradford puts it, centuriation well displayed the arbitrary but methodical qualities in Roman government. With absolute self-assurance and great technical competence, the Romans have imposed the same formal pattern of land division on the well-watered alluvium of the Po Valley as on the near-desert of Tunisia. Even today the forceful imprint of centuriation can be traced across some thousands of square miles on both sides of the central Mediterranean, and it can still stir the imagination by its scale and boldness.[9]

Against this background of the vast transformations of nature in the pagan world, the inroads made in the early centuries of the Christian era were relatively modest. Christianity teaches

8. Plato, *Critias,* transl. by Arnold Toynbee in *Greek Historical Thought,* pp. 146–47.
9. Bradford, John, *Ancient Landscapes* (London, 1957), p. 145.

that man has dominion over nature. St. Benedict himself had cut down the sacred grove at Monte Cassino because it was a survival of pagan worship. And the story of how monks moved into the forested wilderness, and by a combination of work and prayer, had transformed them into cloistered "paradises" is a familiar one. But for a long time man's undisputed power over nature was more a tenet of faith than a fact of experience: to become a realized fact Europe had to wait for the growth of human numbers, for the achievement of greater administrative centralization and for the development and wide application of new technological skills. Fields that were cleared in heavy forests testified to the mediaeval farmer's great capacity for changing his environment: it was a change, however, that must continually be defended against the encroachments of nature. Farmsteads and arable lands multiplied through the Middle Ages at the expense of forests and marshes, but these man-made features lacked the permanence, the geometric order, and the prideful assertion of the human will that one can detect more readily in the Roman road system, aqueducts, and centuriated landholdings. The victory of Christianity over paganism may well have been, as Lynn White says, the greatest psychic revolution in Western culture; but for lack of real, as distinct from theologically postulated, power the full impact of that revolution on ecology was postponed.

III

As to China, Western humanists commonly show bias in favour of that country's Taoist and Buddhist traditions. They like to point out the virtues of the Oriental's quiescent and adaptive approach towards nature in contrast to the aggressive masculinity of Western man. Support for the quiescent view is easily found in the Taoist classics. The *Tao Tê Ching*, for example, has a rather cryptic message of seven characters *(wei wu wei, tzu wu pu chih)* which James Legge has translated as: "When there is this abstinence from action, good order is universal." And Joseph Needham has recently interpreted it to mean: "Let there be no action (contrary to Nature), and there is nothing that will not be well regulated."[10] It is easy to see how these words might appeal to the modern man, who finds in his own environment the all-too-evident consequences of human action "contrary to nature." In another influential Taoist book of much later date *(T'ai shang kan ying p'ien)*, one finds the belief that "even insects and crawling things, herbs and trees, may not be injured." These Taoist texts have been much translated into European languages; the latter, with its injunction against injuring even insects and crawling things, is believed to have had some influence on the thought of Albert Schweitzer.[11]

Another aspect of Chinese attitude towards nature, which has found favour among some Western humanists, is embodied in the concept of *feng-shui* or geomancy. This concept has been aptly defined as "the art of adapting the residences of the living and the dead so as to co-operate and harmonize with the local currents of the cosmic breath."[12] If houses and tombs are not properly located, evil effects would injure the inhabitants and the descendants of those whose bodies lay in the tombs. On the other hand, good siting would favour wealth, health, and happiness. Good siting involves, above all, taking proper note of the forms of hills

10. Needham, Joseph, *Science and Civilisation in China*, vol. II (Cambridge, 1956), p. 69.
11. Schafer, E. H., "The Conservation of Nature under the T'ang Dynasty," *Journ. Econ. and Soc. Hist. of the Orient*, V (1962), 282.
12. Chatley, H., "Feng shui" in *Encyclopaedia Sinica*, ed. by S. Couling (Shanghai, 1917), p. 175. See also Andrew March, "An Appreciation of Chinese Geomancy," *Journ. Asian Studies*, XXVII (1968), 253–67.

and directions of watercourses since these are themselves the outcome of the moulding influences of winds and waters, that is, of *feng-shui;* but in addition one must also consider the heights and forms of buildings, the directions of roads and bridges. A general effect of the belief in *feng-shui* is to encourage a preference for natural curves—for winding paths and for structures that seem to fit into the landscape rather than to dominate it; and at the same time it promoted a distaste for straight lines and geometrical layouts. In this respect it is of interest to note the short life of China's first railway. This was built in 1876 and connected Shanghai with its port of Wu-sung. Although the venture was at first well received, the mood of the local people turned sour after a native was killed by the locomotive. The people in their hostility thought that the railway had offended the principle of *feng-shui.* On 20 October, 1877, the Chinese government closed the railway, and so a symbol of Western progress was temporarily sacrificed to the local currents of the cosmic breath.[13]

An adaptive attitude towards nature has ancient roots in China. It is embodied in folklore, in the philosophical-ethical precepts of Taoism, and later, Buddhism, and it draws support from practical experience: the experience that uncontrolled exploitation of timber, for example, brings hurtful results. In ancient literature one finds here and there evidence of a recognition for the need to regulate the use of resources. Even as early as the Eastern Chou period (eighth century–third century B.C.), deforestation necessitated by the expansion of agriculture and the building of cities seems to have led to an appreciation of the value of trees. In that ancient compendium of songs the *Shi Ching,* we find the sentiment expressed in lines such as these:

13. *Encyclopaedia Sinica,* p. 470.

On the hill were lovely trees,
Both chestnut-trees and plum trees.
Cruel brigands tore them up;
But no one knew of their crime.

Trees were regarded as a blessing. As another poem put it,

So thick grow those oaks
That the people never look for firewood.
Happiness to our lord!
May the spirits always have rewards for him.[14]

In the *Chou Li*—a work which was probably compiled in the third century B.C., but may well include earlier material—we find mentioned two classes of officials whose duties were concerned with conservation. One was the *Shan-yu,* inspector of mountains, and the other the *Lin-heng,* inspector of forests. The inspectors of mountains were charged with the care of forests in the mountains. They saw to it that certain species were preserved, and in other ways enforced conservation practices. Thus trees could only be cut by the common people at certain times; those on the south side in the middle of winter and those on the north side in the middle of summer. At other seasons the people were permitted to cut wood in times of urgent need, such as when coffins had to be made or dykes strengthened, but even then certain areas could not be touched. The inspectors of forests (in the *Lin-heng* office) had similar duties. Their authority covered the forests that lay below the mountains.[15] Another ancient literary reference to conservation practice was in the

14. *Shi Ching,* transl. by Arthur Waley as *The Book of Songs* (New York, 1960), pp. 138, 213.
15. *Chou Li,* transl. by E. Biot as *Le Tcheou-li* (Paris, 1851), vol. I, 371–74.

Mencius. The sage advised King Huai of Liang that he would not lack for wood if he allowed the people to cut trees only at the proper time.[16]

Through Chinese history perspicacious officials have from time to time warned against the dire consequences of deforestation. A scholar of the late Ming dynasty reported on Shan-hsi, a province in North China: "At the beginning of the reign of Chia-ching" (1522–66), he wrote, "people vied with each other to build houses, and wood from the southern mountains was cut without a year's rest. The natives took advantage of the barren mountain surface and converted it into farms. . . . If heaven sends down a torrent, there is nothing to obstruct the flow of water. In the morning it falls on the southern mountains; in the evening, when it reaches the plains, its angry waves swell in volume and break embankments causing frequent changes in the course of the river."[17]

Deforestation was deplored by the late Ming scholars not only because of its effect on stream flow and on the quality of the soil in the lowlands, but also—interestingly enough—because of their belief that the forests on mountain ridges were effective in slowing down the horse-riding barbarians. As one scholar put it, "I saw the fact that what the country relies on as strategically important is the mountain, and what the mountain relies on as a screen to prevent advance are the trees."[18] There was also recognition of the aesthetics of forested mountains. Wu-tai mountains in northern Shan-hsi, for example,

16. *Mencius,* Bk. I, pt. 1, 3:3.
17. Chi, Ch'ao-ting, *Key Economic Areas in Chinese History* (New York, 1963), p. 22.
18. Gazetteer (1596) written by Chen Teng and translated by W. C. Lowdermilk, and D. R. Wickes, *History of Soil Use in the Wu T'ai Shan Area,* Monog., Roy. Asiatic Soc., NCB, 1938, p. 8.

were famous everywhere. But the question was asked: since they have become almost bare, what remained to keep them famous?

These brief notes suggest that there existed in China an old tradition of forest care. Officials encouraged the practice but the people engaged in it on their own initiative when it did not conflict with the urgent needs of the moment. Nearly forty years ago, the American conservationist W. C. Lowdermilk noted how thousands of acres in An-hui and Ho-non were planted with pine from local nurseries, a practice he recognized as ancient and independent of the modern forestry movement. Lowdermilk also found that the North China plain "actually exports considerable quantities of logs of *Paulownia tomentosa* to Japan and poplar *(Populus tomentosa)* to match factories. It is true that no forests are to be found in this plain, but each village has its trees, which are grown according to a system."[19]

In Communist China trees are extensively planted to control soil erosion, in answer to pressing economic needs but also for aesthetic reasons. Roadside planting, a practice dating back to the Eastern Chou period, uses the "traditional" trees *(Populus simonii, Pinus tabulaeformis, Salix babylonica, S. matsudana, Aesculus chinensis, Ulmus parvifolia),* but in particular the poplars. Afforestation proceeds in villages, and most conspicuously, in cities, new suburbs, and industrial districts where the trees hide a great deal of the raw ugliness of new construction.[20]

IV

Thus far I have sketched what may indeed be called the "official" line on Chinese attitude towards environment; it is widely

19. Lowdermilk, W. C., "Forestry in Denuded China," *Ann., Amer. Acad. Pol. Soc. Sci.,* CLII (1930), 137.
20. Richardson, S. D., *Forestry in Communist China* (Baltimore, 1966), pp. 152–53.

publicized and commonly accepted. There is however another strain: the enlightened memorials to the emperor on the need for the conservation of resources are in themselves clear evidence of the follies that have already been committed. Unlike the Western man of letters the geographer is usually aware of China's frequent mistreatment of nature. He perceives that country, not through the refined sentiments of Taoist philosophy, Neo-Confucianism, and Oswald Siren, but through the bleak reports of Mallory, Lowdermilk, and Thorp. Deforestation and erosion on the one hand, the building of cities and rice terraces on the other are the common foci of his attention rather than landscape painting or poetry contests in the cool precincts of a garden. The two images of reality complement each other: in an obvious but not trite sense, civilization is the exercise of human power over nature, which in turn may lead to the aesthetic appreciation of nature. Philosophy, nature poetry, gardens, and orderly countryside are products of civilization, but so equally are the deforested mountains, the clogged streams, and, within the densely packed, walled cities, the political intrigue.

If animistic belief and Taoist nature philosophy lie at the back of an adaptive attitude towards nature, what conceptions and ideals—we may ask—have encouraged the Chinese, through their long history, to engage in gigantic transformation of environment—whether this be expressed positively in huge works of construction or negatively in deforested mountains? Several ancient beliefs and conceptions may be recognized and they, individually or together, have allowed the Chinese to express the "male" principle in human nature. Consider, for example, the fact that one of the greatest culture heroes of China was Yu, the legendary founder of the Hsia dynasty. He was famed primarily for his magnificent deeds: He "opened up the rivers of the Nine Provinces and fixed the outlets of the nine marshes"; he brought peace and order to the lands of Hsia and his achievements were of an enduring kind which benefited succeeding dynasties.[21] Chinese rulers were bidden to imitate the ancient culture heroes, and one way to imitate them was to ensure order and prosperity by large-scale engineering works. Another ancient idea of importance to the "male" principle of dominance was to see in the earthly environment a model of the cosmos. The regular motions of the stars were to be translated architecturally and ritually to space and time on earth. The walled city oriented to the cardinal directions, the positioning of the twelve city gates, the location of the royal compound and the alignment of the principal axial street were given a geometric pattern that reflected the order to be found in heaven. The key concept was built on the related notions of rectilinearity, order, and rectitude. This key concept acquired architectural and social forms which were then imposed on earth, for the earth itself lacked paradigms of perfect order. Indeed the experience of mountains and waters has led to such unaggressive prescriptions as the need to observe and placate the spirits of the earth, the need for man to understand the balance of forces in nature, to contemplate this harmony and to adapt himself to it. By contrast, the observation of the stars has inspired such masculine attitudes as geometric order, hierarchy, and authoritarian control over earth and men.

The two outlooks—celestial and terrestrial, masculine and feminine—are not easy to reconcile. Events in heaven affect events on earth but not in any obvious or dependable way: abnormal floods and droughts have traditionally been taken as warnings by those who derive their power from astronomy. Tension, if not contradiction, is also revealed when these two ideas find architectural and geographical substance. The construction of Ch'ang-an in the Sui and T'ang dynasties illustrates the triumph of the cosmic principle of order and rectilinearity

21. Ssu-ma Ch'ien, *Shi Chi,* chap. 29.

over the earth principle of complex harmony and natural lines. Ch'ang-an was laid on new ground and on an unprecedented scale. The site in the Wei Ho valley was chosen for functional reasons but also because of its great historical links: the site received the sanction of the great men and deeds in the past. Geomantic properties of the site were studied; however, unlike villages and rural roads the topographical character of the region seems to have made little impact on the city's fundamental design. Astronomers had an important role in the laying out of the city: they measured the shadow of the noon sun on successive days and observed the North Star by night in order to arrive at accurate alignments of the city walls to the four directions.[22] In the course of building Ch'ang-an, which had an enclosed area of 31 square miles, villages were levelled and trees uprooted; broad straight avenues were laid out and then rows of trees planted. Thus, despite the geomantic gestures, in Ch'ang-an the superposition of man's and heaven's order on natural terrain was complete. Or rather not quite complete, if we accept the charming story of why one great old locust tree was not in line. It had been retained from the old landscape because the chief architect had sat under it as he supervised the construction, and a special order from the emperor in honour of his architect spared it from being felled.[23]

V

The natural environment of both Mediterranean Europe and China has been vastly transformed by man: constructively in the building of cities and roads, in the extension of arable land and

22. Wright, A. F., "Symbolism and Functions: Reflections on Changan and Other Great Cities," *Journ. Asian Studies,* XXIV (1965), 670.
23. Wu, N. I., *Chinese and Indian Architecture* (New York, 1963), p. 38.

the introduction of new crops; destructively in deforestation and erosion. Of any long-settled, thoroughly civilized part of the world, we can draw up a list of forces and the motives for their use that would more or less account for the transformation of the biotic mantle. Such lists may well agree in fundamentals: fire is widely used to clear vegetation; the forest is cleared to create more grazing and arable land; timber is needed for the construction of palaces, houses, and ships, for domestic and industrial fuel, or as raw material for paper mills. Then again the forest is pushed back because it may shelter dangerous wild animals or provide hiding places for bandits. Naturally, the means at hand and the motives for using them vary from region to region: in contrast to the Mediterranean world, for example, China's vegetation suffered less from sheep and goats, and less from the enormous demands of shipbuilding which flourished with the Mediterranean maritime powers. China's forests, on the other hand, suffered more from the demands of city building and the need for domestic fuel.

To illustrate further the kinds of force that work against conservation practices in China, consider some of the causes of deforestation. One is the ancient practice of burning trees in order to deprive dangerous animals of their hiding places. There exists a passage in the *Mencius* of how in ancient times the luxuriant vegetation sheltered so many wild beasts that men were endangered. The great minister Shun of legendary repute ordered Yih to use fire, and "Yih set fire to, and consumed the forests and vegetation on the mountains and in the marshes, so that the birds and beasts fled away to hide themselves."[24] Even in the early decades of the twentieth century non-Chinese tribes in Kuang-hsi and Kuei-chou provinces are known to burn forests to drive away tigers and leopards; and in North China, in

24. *Mencius,* Bk. III, pt. 1, 4:7.

such long-settled areas as central Shen-hsi province, fires were ostensibly started by Chinese farmers for no other purpose. It is not always easy to establish the real reason for setting fire to forest. When asked, the farmers may say that it is to clear land for cultivation, although the extent of burning far exceeds the need for this purpose; or it is to leave fewer places in which bandits may hide; or to encourage the growth of small-sized sprouts in the burnt over area, which would then save the farmers the labour of splitting wood![25] The last reason tends to upset any residual illusion we may have of the Chinese farmer's benign attitude towards nature. A fire can of course also be started accidentally. A risk that is special to the Chinese is the forest fire caused by the burning of paper money at the grave mounds, which, in the rugged parts of the South, are commonly located beyond the fields and at the edge of the forested hills.

Forests in North China were depleted in the past for the making of charcoal as an industrial fuel. Robert Hartwell has shown how, from the tenth century onward the expanding metallic industries had swallowed up many hundreds of thousands of tons of charcoal each year, as did the manufacture of salt, alum, bricks, tiles, and liquor.[26] By the Sung dynasty (A.D. 960–1279) the demand for wood and charcoal as both household and industrial fuel had reached a level such that the timber resources of the country could no longer meet it; the result was the increasing substitution of coal for wood and charcoal.

An enormous amount of timber was needed in the construction of the old Chinese cities, probably more than that required

25. Reported by A. N. Steward and S. Y. Cheo in "Geographical and Ecological Notes on Botanical Explorations in Kwangsi Province, China," *Nanking Journ.*, v (1935), 174.
26. Hartwell, R., "A Revolution in the Chinese Iron and Coal Industries during the Northern Sung, 960–1126 A.D.," *Journ. Asian Studies,* XXI (1962), 159.

in building Western cities of comparable size. One reason for this lies in the dependence of traditional Chinese architecture on timber as the basic structural material. Mountains may be stripped of their cover in the construction of a large palace.[27] And if a large palace required much timber, a whole city would require much more, especially if it were of the size of Ch'ang-an, capital of T'ang dynasty, and Hang-chou, capital of the southern Sung dynasty. Both had populations of more than a million people. The great expansion in the size of Hang-chou in the thirteenth century led to the deforestation of the neighbouring hills for construction timber. The demand for timber was such that some farmers gave up rice cultivation for forestry.[28] Cities in which houses were so largely made of wood ran the constant danger of demolition by fire; and this was especially true of the southern metropolises where the streets tended to be narrow. The necessity of rebuilding after fire put further strain on timber resources. But of even greater consequence than the accidental burning of parts of cities was the deliberate devastation of whole cities in times of upheaval, when rebels or nomadic invaders toppled a dynasty. The succeeding phase of reconstruction was normally achieved in quick time by armies of men who made ruthless inroads upon the forest.

VI

The theme we have yet to trace is the involved interplay between environmental attitude and environmental behaviour, between the philosophy identified with a people and the actions that

27. See L. S. Yang, *Les aspects économiques des travaux publics dans la Chine impériale,* Collège de France, 1964. p. 37.
28. Gernet, (n. 1), p. 114.

people may undertake. Besides the more glaring contradictions of professed ideal and actual practice, there exist also the unsuspected ironies: these derive from the fact that the benign institutions of a complex society, no less than the exploitative, are not always able to foresee all the consequences of their inherent character and action. For example, Buddhism in China is at least partly responsible for the preservation of trees around temple compounds, for the islands of green in an otherwise denuded landscape; on the other hand, Buddhism introduced to China the idea of the cremation of the dead; and from the tenth to the fourteenth century the practice of cremation was sufficiently common in the southeastern coastal provinces to have had an effect on the timber resources of that area.[29] The researches of E. H. Schafer provide us with another illustration of irony in Chinese life; for it would seem that the most civilized of arts was responsible for the deforestation of much of North China. The art was that of writing which required soot for the making of black ink. The soot came from burnt pine. And, as Schafer put it, "Even before T'ang times, the ancient pines of the mountains of Shan-tung had been reduced to carbon, and now the busy brushes of the vast T'ang bureaucracy were rapidly bringing baldness to the T'a-hang Mountains between Shansi and Hopei."[30]

VII

I began by noting the contrast between the European formal garden and the Chinese naturalistic garden, and then suggested that these human achievements probably required comparable

29. Moule, A. C., *Quinsai* (Cambridge, 1957), p. 51.
30. Schafer, (n. 11), pp. 299–300.

amounts of nature modification. To compare artworks and construction projects on the basis of the quantitative changes made on the environment is a useful exercise in so far as we wish to emphasize the role of man as a force for change along with other geophysical forces; but it is only the beginning in the interpretation of the meaning of these works and how they reflect cultural attitudes. It seems to me valid to see the European garden as an extension of the house: in the development of the European garden some of the formality and values of the house are taken outdoors in the form of courtyards, terraces, formal parterres, and avenues, and now the smooth, carpet-like lawn. The lawn displays the house; its sloping surfaces are a pedestal for the house. The Chinese garden, on the other hand, reflects a totally different philosophy from the orthogonal rectitude of the traditional Chinese house. In stepping through a circular gate, from the rectangular courtyard into the curvilinear forms of the garden, one enters a different world. Perhaps something of the difference in attitude towards outdoor spaces is retained to the present day. Simone de Beauvoir notes how a French family picnic is often an elaborate affair involving the transportation of a considerable portion of the household goods outdoors: it is not always a harmonious event for whatever tension that may exist in the house is carried to the less organized natural environment where it is exacerbated by entanglement with flies, fishing rods, and spilled strawberry jam. In Communist China, de Beauvoir spent an afternoon (1955) in the playgrounds of the Summer Palace outside Peking. She captures the peace of the scene with an anecdote: "In the middle of the lake I see a little boat: in it a young woman is lying down peacefully asleep while two youngsters are frisking about and playing with the oars. Our boatman cups his hands. 'Hey!' he calls. 'Look out for those kids!' The woman rubs her eyes, she smiles, picks up the oars, and shows the children how they work."[31]

31. de Beauvoir, Simone, *The Long March* (Cleveland, 1958), p. 77.

Franciscan Conservation versus Benedictine Stewardship

RENÉ DUBOS

History is replete with ecological disasters; the most flourishing lands of antiquity seem to have been under a malediction. Mesopotamia, Persia, Egypt, West Pakistan were once the sites of civilizations which remained powerful and wealthy for great periods of time but are now among the poorest areas of the world. Their lands are barren deserts, many of their ancient cities abandoned, most of their people so poor, malnourished, and diseased that they have no memory or even awareness of their magnificent past. Since the same situation is true for much of India, China, Southeast Asia, and Latin America, it would seem that, contrary to certain views, all civilizations are mortal.

Civil strife, warfare, famine, and disease certainly contributed to the demise of ancient Eastern civilizations, but the desolate appearance of their lands today would seem to indicate that the primary cause of the decline was the depletion of the soil caused by prolonged occupation by large numbers of people. Exhaus-

SOURCE: "Franciscan Conservation versus Benedictine Stewardship" is reprinted from *A God Within* by René Dubos by permission of Charles Scribner's Sons.

tion or destruction of water resources probably followed and dealt the final blow. Babylonian civilization, for example, disappeared after its system of irrigation was destroyed by the Mongols, but its environment had begun to degenerate long before this final disaster.[1]

The English archaeologist Sir Mortimer Wheeler has examined in detail the fate of Mohenjo Daro, the archaeologically famous city-civilization that flourished from 2500 to 1500 B.C. on the plains of the Indus River in present-day Pakistan. This civilization, which prospered some four thousand years ago, at the same time as Mesopotamian and Egyptian civilizations, differed from them in its architecture, art, and technology. Like them, however, it disappeared because, in Wheeler's words, it was "steadily wearing out its landscape."[2] In modern ecological jargon this means that its environment was being destroyed by overuse or misuse. Pessimists have therefore much historical evidence for their thesis that civilizations inevitably ruin their environments.

There is, however, another side to the question. The American geographer C. O. Sauer is of the opinion that "the worn-out parts of the world are the recent settlements, not the lands of old civilizations."[3] For more than a thousand years, Japanese agriculture has remained highly productive without decreasing the fertility of the soil or spoiling the beauty of the landscape. In Western Europe also, as mentioned elsewhere, many areas opened to agriculture by the Neolithic settlers remain fertile

1. Paul B. Sears, "Climate and Civilization," in H. Shapley (ed.), *Climatic Change* (Cambridge, Mass.: Harvard University Press, 1953), 44.
2. Quoted in Raymond Nace, "Arrogance Toward the Landscape: A Problem in Water Planning," *Bulletin of the Atomic Scientists,* 25 (1969), 14.
3. Carl O. Sauer, *Land and Life* (Berkeley, Calif.: University of California Press, 1963), 148.

today after several thousand years of almost continuous use. This immense duration of certain cultivated landscapes contributes a sense of tranquility to many parts of the Old World; it inspires confidence that mankind can survive its present ordeals and learn to manage the land for the sake of the future.

These contrasting views of the relationships between civilization and the land may not be as incompatible as they appear. All the great Eastern civilizations which wore out their soil were located in and around semiarid and arid zones. Under such climatic conditions, which prevail over approximately 35 percent of the world's land mass, productive agriculture depends upon irrigation, and damage to the soil can be rapid and almost irreversible. In contrast, Western Europe, Japan, and certain other parts of Asia are blessed with a greater and especially a more constant rainfall, which enables their soils to recover fairly rapidly after they have been damaged by ecological mismanagement. Climatic conditions, however, cannot account entirely for the fate of the world's civilizations. They do not explain the sudden disappearance of the Maya, Khmer, and other great civilizations which once flourished in humid countries. In Mexico, the end of the Teotihuacan culture occurred suddenly, around A.D. 800, during a moist period. The primary cause was probably the fact that the protective forests of the region had been cut to provide fuel for the extensive burning of lime. The erosion that ensued, coupled with the destructive effects of cultivation, was apparently sufficient to offset the blessings of returning moisture. Ecological mismanagement was also responsible for the deterioration of agriculture around the Mediterranean basin in the ancient world and is now creating similar problems in many temperate regions, including the United States. The land has remained fertile under intense cultivation only where farmers have used it according to sound ecological principles.

Unwise management of nature or of technology can destroy civilization in any climate and land, under any political system.

Environmental degradation in the modern world is commonly traced to technological excesses, but the roots of the problem go far deeper. When George Perkins Marsh visited the Near East in the middle of the nineteenth century, he was shocked to find deserted cities, silted harbors, and wastelands instead of flourishing civilizations. Technology could not then be blamed for soil turned barren, forests destroyed, and ancient bodies of water replaced by salt and sand flats. Marsh properly concluded that ecological errors had led to the deterioration of agriculture in the Mediterranean countries, and he recognized also that good agricultural practices had preserved the quality of the land in other parts of the world. His book *Man and Nature,* first published in 1864 and revised in 1874 under the new title *The Earth as Modified by Human Action,* advocated conservation practices but chiefly from the agricultural point of view.[4]

While Marsh emphasized the quality of agricultural lands, another aspect of ecological concern was taking shape in the United States—the efforts to save the quality of nature. One of the most articulate spokesmen of the new movement was the American ecologist Aldo Leopold (1887–1948), whose primary commitment was to wildlife and to undisturbed wilderness. Leopold advocated an ecological conscience in all aspects of man's relation with nature and as one of the founders of the Wilderness Society was influential in securing government approval for the protection of America's first wilderness area at the head of the Gila River in New Mexico. He preached a "land ethic" in his

4. George P. Marsh, *The Earth as Modified by Human Action: A New Edition of "Man and Nature"* (New York: Scribner, Armstrong & Co., 1874).

book *A Sand County Almanac,* which has become the Holy Writ of American conservationists.[5]

Marsh's influence was not great, probably because he wrote at a time when the methods of modern agriculture were producing enormous increases of crop yields, and his teachings therefore seemed irrelevant. In contrast, Leopold rapidly gained a large following because the obvious damage done to nature by the new technologies had created a public mood receptive to his plea for a new ethic of man's relation to nature.

A curious expression of the present public concern for the environmental crisis has been the theory, which became academically fashionable during the 1960s, that the Judeo-Christian tradition is responsible for the desecration of nature in the Western world. This view seems to have been publicized for the first time around 1950 by the Zen Buddhist Daisetz Suzuki.[6] But it was given academic glamor by Lynn White, Jr., professor of history at the University of California at Los Angeles, in a much publicized lecture entitled, "The Historical Roots of Our Ecologic Crisis."[7] It is a measure of its popular success that this lecture has been reproduced *in extenso,* not only in learned and popular magazines but also in *The Oracle,* the multicolored, now defunct journal of the hippie culture in San Francisco. Whether valid or not, White's thesis demands attention because it has become an article of faith for many conservationists, ecologists, economists, and even theologians. The thesis runs approximately as follows.

5. Aldo Leopold, *A Sand County Almanac and Sketches Here and There* (New York: Oxford University Press, 1949).

6. Clarence J. Glacken, *Traces on the Rhodian Shore* (Richmond, Calif.: University of California Press, 1967), 494.

7. Lynn White, Jr., "The Historical Roots of Our Ecologic Crisis," *Science,* 155 (1967), 1203–1207.

The ancient Oriental and Greco-Roman religions took it for granted that animals, trees, rivers, mountains, and other natural objects can have spiritual significance just like men and therefore deserve respect. According to the Judeo-Christian religions, in contrast, man is apart from nature. The Jews adopted monotheism with a distinctly anthropomorphic concept of God. The Christians developed this trend still further by shifting religion toward an exclusive concern with human beings. It is explicitly stated in Chapter 1 of Genesis that man was shaped in the image of God and given dominion over creation; this has provided the excuse for a policy of exploitation of nature, regardless of consequences. Christianity developed, of course, along different lines in different parts of the world. In its Eastern forms its ideal was the saint dedicated to prayer and contemplation, whereas in its Western forms it was the saint dedicated to action. Because of this geographical difference in Christian attitudes, the most profound effects of man's impact on nature have been in the countries of Western civilization. To a large extent, furthermore, modern technology is the expression of the Judeo-Christian belief that man has a rightful dominion over nature. Biblical teachings thus account for the fact that Western man has had no scruples in using the earth's resources for his own selfish interests or in exploring the moon to satisfy his curiosity, even if this means the raping of nature and the contamination of the lunar surface.

Since the roots of the environmental crisis are so largely religious, the remedy must also be essentially religious: "I personally doubt," White writes, "that ecologic backlashes can be avoided simply by applying to our problems more science and more technology." For this reason, he suggests that the only solution may be a return to the humble attitude of the early Franciscans. Francis of Assisi worshiped all aspects of nature and believed in the virtue of humility, not only for the individual person but for man as a species; we should try to follow in his footsteps, so as to "depose man from his monarchy over creation, and abandon our aggressive attitude toward Nature." "I propose Francis as a patron saint of ecologists," is the conclusion of White's essay.[8]

In my opinion, the theory that Judeo-Christian attitudes are responsible for the development of technology and for the ecological crisis is at best a historical half-truth. Erosion of the land, destruction of animal and plant species, excessive exploitation of natural resources, and ecological disasters are not peculiar to the Judeo-Christian tradition and to scientific technology. At all times, and all over the world, man's thoughtless interventions into nature have had a variety of disastrous consequences or at least have changed profoundly the complexion of nature.

The process began some ten thousand years ago, long before the Bible was written.[9] A dramatic extinction of several species of large mammals and terrestrial birds occurred at the very beginning of the Neolithic period, coincident with the expansion of agricultural man. His eagerness to protect cultivated fields and flocks may account for the attitude "if it moves, kill it," which is rooted deep in folk traditions over much of the world. Nor was the destruction of large animals motivated only by utilitarian reasons. In Egypt the pharaohs and the nobility arranged for large numbers of beasts to be driven into compounds where they were trapped and then shot with arrows. The Assyri-

8. Ibid., 1207.

9. See John D. Buffington, "Predation, Competition, and Pleistocene Megafauna Extinction," *BioScience,* 21 (1971), 167–170; Robert Gordis, "Judaism and the Spoliation of Nature," *Congress Bi-Weekly,* April 2, 1971, 9–12; Daniel A. Guthrie, "Primitive Man's Relationship to Nature," *BioScience,* 21 (1971), 721–723; Joe Ben Wheat, "A Paleo-Indian Bison Kill," *Scientific American,* 216 (1967), 44–52; Richard T. Wright, "Responsibility for the Ecological Crisis," *BioScience,* 21 (1970), 851–853; and "Here We Go Again," *Scientific American,* 224 (1971), 59.

ans, too, were as vicious destroyers of animals—lions and elephants, for example—as they were of men. Ancient hunting practices greatly reduced the populations of some large animal species and in some cases led to their eradication. This destructive process has continued throughout historical times, not only in the regions peripheral to the eastern Mediterranean, but also in other parts of the world. In Australia, the nomadic aborigines with their fire sticks had far-reaching effects on the environment. Early explorers commented upon the aborigines' widespread practice of setting fires, which under the semiarid conditions of Australia drastically altered the vegetation cover, caused erosion, and destroyed much of the native fauna. Huge tracts of forest land were thus converted into open grasslands and the populations of large marsupials were greatly reduced.

Plato's statement in *Critias* of his belief that Greece was eroded before his time as a result of deforestation and overgrazing has already been mentioned [in an earlier chapter]. Erosion resulting from human activities probably caused the end of the Teotihuacan civilization in ancient Mexico. Early men, aided especially by that most useful and most noxious of all animals, the Mediterranean goat, were probably responsible for more deforestation and erosion than all the bulldozers of the Judeo-Christian world.

Nor is there reason to believe that Oriental civilizations have been more respectful of nature than Judeo-Christian civilizations. As shown by the British scientist and historian Joseph Needham, China was far ahead of Europe in scientific and technological development until the seventeenth century A.D. and used technology on a massive and often destructive scale.[10] Many passages in T'ang and Sung poetry indicate that the bar-

10. Joseph Needham, *Science and Civilisation in China,* 4 vols. (Cambridge: Cambridge University Press, 1954–1962).

ren hills of central and northern China were once heavily forested, and there is good reason to believe that, there as elsewhere, treelessness and soil erosion are results of fires and overgrazing. Even the Buddhists contributed largely to the deforestation of Asia in order to build their temples; it has been estimated that in some areas they have been responsible for much more than half of the timber consumption.[11]

The Chinese attitude of respect for nature probably arose, in fact, as a response to the damage done in antiquity. Furthermore, this respect does not go as far as artistic and poetical expressions would indicate. The classic nature poets of China write as if they had achieved identification with the cosmos, but in reality most of them were retired bureaucrats living on estates in which nature was carefully trimmed and managed by gardeners. In Japan also, the beautifully artificial gardens and oddly shaped pine trees could hardly be regarded as direct expressions of nature; they constitute rather a symbolic interpretation of an intellectual attitude toward scenery. Wildlife has been so severely reduced in modern Japan that sparrows and swallows are the only kinds of birds remaining of the dozens of species that used to pass through Tokyo a century ago.

One of the best-documented examples of ecological mismanagement in the ancient world is the progressive destruction of the groves of cedars and cypresses that in the past were the glory of Lebanon. The many references to these noble evergreen groves in ancient inscriptions and in the Old Testament reveal that the Egyptian pharaohs and the kings of Assyria or Babylon carried off enormous amounts of the precious timber for the temples and palaces of their capital cities.[12] In a taunt against

11. Yi-Fu Tuan, "Our Treatment of the Environment in Ideal and Actuality," *American Scientist,* 58 (1970), 248.
12. Nina Jidejian, *Byblos Through the Ages* (Beirut: Dar El Machreq, 1968).

Nebuchadnezzar, king of Babylon, the prophet Isaiah refers to the destructive effects of these logging expeditions. The Roman emperors, especially Hadrian, extended still further the process of deforestation. Today the few surviving majestic cedars are living testimony to what the coniferous forests of Lebanon were like before the ruthless exploitation which long preceded the Judeo-Christian and technological age.

All over the globe and at all times in the past, men have pillaged nature and disturbed the ecological equilibrium, usually out of ignorance, but also because they have always been more concerned with immediate advantages than with long-range goals. Moreover, they could not foresee that they were preparing for ecological disasters, nor did they have a real choice of alternatives. If men are more destructive now than they were in the past, it is because there are more of them and because they have at their command more powerful means of destruction, not because they have been influenced by the Bible. In fact, the Judeo-Christian peoples were probably the first to develop on a large scale a pervasive concern for land management and an ethic of nature.

Among the great Christian teachers, none is more identified with an ethic of nature than Francis of Assisi (1182?–1226), who treated all living things and inanimate objects as if they were his brothers and sisters. His tradition has continued to express itself in many forms among Judeo-Christian people, as for example in the philosophical concept that all living things can be arranged in a continuous series—the Great Chain of Being;[13] in Albert Schweitzer's reverence for life; in the semitranscendental

13. Arthur O. Lovejoy, *The Great Chain of Being* (Cambridge, Mass.: Harvard University Press, 1936).

utterances of writers such as Wordsworth, Thoreau, or Walt Whitman. The Darwinian theory of evolution provided a scientific basis for the intuitive belief in the universal brotherhood of all living things. Most modern men have come to accept or at least to tolerate the thought, so disturbing a century ago, that man belongs to a natural line of descent which includes all animals and plants. It is not unlikely that the Franciscan worship of nature, in its various philosophical, scientific, and religious forms, has played some part in the emergence of the doctrine of conservation in the countries of Western civilization and its rapid spread during the past century.

While it is easy to believe that wilderness should be preserved wherever possible, the reasons generally given to advocate the maintenance of undisturbed ecological systems and the preservation of endangered species are not entirely convincing. Despite what the conservationists say, nature will go on even if whooping cranes, condors, or redwoods are exterminated, just as it has gone on after the extinction of millions of other species that have vanished from the earth in the course of time. The fossil beds with their myriad of long-vanished forms testify to the fact that man is not the first agency to alter the biological composition of the earth.

Environments which are being upset by smogs, pesticides, or strip mining are not destroyed thereby; they will become different by evolving in directions determined by these challenges. We may not like the consequences of these changes for ethical, esthetic, or economic reasons, but it is nevertheless certain that the disturbed environments will eventually achieve some new kind of biologic status, as has been the case in the past after all great ecological disasters.

The advance of continental ice sheets during the Pleistocene destroyed much of the flora and fauna and in many places removed the soil down to the bedrock. But nature is so resilient that the rocks made barren by the glaciers eventually acquired a new flora and new fauna. Destruction always results in a different creation. The American chestnut *(Castanea dentata),* which had been a dominant member of the forest in the eastern United States, was all but eradicated following the accidental introduction of a fungus from Asia in 1906; today, the dead chestnut trees are turning into humus, and their place in the forest canopy has been taken by several species of oak.

In 1883, the small island of Krakatoa, situated between Java and Sumatra, was the site of a tremendous volcanic eruption. The explosive force was so great that as much as two-thirds of the island was blown away. The accompanying tidal wave caused immense damage along all the nearby coasts, and volcanic dust spread over vast portions of the globe. A careful search through the island, one year after the eruption, revealed only one spider and a few blades of grass. But twenty-five years later, 202 species of animals were found in the course of a three-day search. Fifty years after the eruption, the biological recovery had gone so far that 880 animal species could be counted and a small forest covered much of the island. Most of the new forms of life had come from Java and Sumatra.[14] The Pacific atolls of Bikini and Eniwetok, which were pulverized by multiple nuclear blasts between 1946 and 1958, similarly had returned to an almost normal state in 1964, despite the destruction of their topsoil.

Changes occur even under natural conditions, because nature continuously evolves. As pointed out by C. O. Sauer, the classical concept of "ecologic climax" is a postulate which tends to

14. Anthony Smith, *The Seasons: Life and Its Rhythms* (New York: Harcourt Brace Jovanovich, 1970), 162, 166.

replace reality. Climax assumes the end of change, but the ecological reality is a dynamic state; the biological equilibrium is never reached because natural and human influences continuously alter the interplay between the various components of the ecosystem.[15]

Final or stable communities are exceptional in nature and they are impossible wherever there is human activity. Every form of agriculture, even the most primitive, involves the creation of artificial ecosystems. Since most of the temperate world has now been transformed by man, the balance of nature is at best an artificial and static concept unrelated to the conditions that prevail in most of the world.

Although the need to maintain the balance of nature cannot provide a valid case for conservation, there are other strong reasons for protecting environmental quality and preserving as much wilderness as possible. Some of these reasons were cogently stated in the 1860s by George P. Marsh:

> *It is desirable that some large and easily accessible region of American soil should remain as far as possible in its primitive condition, at once a museum for the instruction of students, a garden for the recreation of lovers of nature, and an asylum where indigenous trees . . . plants . . . beasts may dwell and perpetuate their kind.*[16]

It has now become obvious that the pollution of rivers and lakes is creating grave economic problems because the United States is coming close to a shortage of water for home and industrial needs. Polluted air damages buildings and vegetation;

15. Carl O. Sauer, *Agricultural Origins and Dispersals: The Domestication of Animals and Foodstuffs* (Cambridge, Mass.: M.I.T. Press, 1969), 15.
16. Quoted in Max Nicholson, *The Environmental Revolution* (New York: McGraw-Hill, 1970), 168.

automobile exhausts kill evergreens and dogwoods along the highways, as well as the celebrated pines of Rome. In all its forms, air pollution is deleterious to human health and increases medical problems.

A scientific justification for taking a conservative attitude toward changes in nature is that the long-range outcome of human interventions into natural ecosystems cannot be predicted with certainty. Past experience has shown that many of these interventions have resulted in unforeseen ecological disturbances, often disastrous for man himself.

Another justification is that the progressive loss of wilderness decreases biological diversity. This in turn renders ecological systems less stable and less likely to remain suitable for a variety of species, including man. Conservation of natural systems is the best guarantee against irrevocable loss of diversity and the simplest way to minimize ecological disasters. Consider what might happen if—as has been seriously suggested by some "experts" in lumbering companies—native forests were completely replaced by artificial forests. This could certainly be accomplished by planting seedlings of the few desired species and growing them under controlled conditions with generous use of fertilizers and protective sprays. The artificial forest would probably be economically profitable for years or decades, but if such tree farms became victims of infection or other ecological accidents, and if there were no sizable natural forest communities left in the climatic and soil regions where the artificial ones had been established, starting the reforestation process anew would be extremely difficult. Undisturbed native marshes, prairies, deserts, and forests are at present the best assurance against the potential hazards inherent in the truncated, oversimplified ecosystems that are being created by the monocultures of a few strains selected for specialized properties, especially in view of the fact that these strains require massive use of chemical fertilizers, plant hormones, pesticides, and other synthetic products. As the American ecologist David Ehrenfeld stated in *Biological Conservation,* the prospect of vast blighted zones choked with weeds and scarred by erosion is more than a Wellsian fantasy.[17]

Above and beyond the economic and ecological reasons for conservation, there are esthetic and moral ones which are even more compelling. The statement that the earth is our mother is more than a sentimental platitude, since, as I have said elsewhere, we are shaped by the earth. The characteristics of the environment in which we develop condition our biological and mental being and the quality of our life. Were it only for selfish reasons, therefore, we must maintain variety and harmony in nature. Fortunately, as ecologists have estimated, the amount of ecological reserves needed in North America approximates ten million acres, which is far less than 1 percent of the total land area of the continent. But even if the economic impact were greater than this statement suggests, the conservation of wilderness would be justified for a number of spiritual values on which a dollar sign cannot be put. The ever-increasing popularity of the national parks, the presence of aquariums and plants in city apartments, may indicate that pigeons, dogs, cats, and even people do not suffice to make a completely satisfying world. Our separation from the rest of the natural world leaves us with a subconscious feeling that we must retain some contact with wilderness and with as wide a range of living things as possible. The national parks contribute a value that transcends economic considerations and may play a role similar to that of Stonehenge, the pyramids, Greek temples, Roman ruins, Gothic

17. David Ehrenfeld, *Biological Conservation* (New York: Holt, Rinehart and Winston, 1970).

cathedrals, the Williamsburg restoration, Gettysburg battlefield, or the holy sites of various religions.

Ian McMillan, a California naturalist, has written of the struggle to save the California condor: "The real importance of saving such things as condors is not so much that we need condors as that we need to save them. We need to exercise and develop the human attributes required in saving condors; for these are the attributes so necessary in working out our own survival."[18] Conservation is based on human value systems; its deepest significance is in the human situation and the human heart. Saving marshlands and redwoods does not need biological justification any more than does opposing callousness and vandalism.[19] The cult of wilderness is not a luxury; it is a necessity for the protection of humanized nature and for the preservation of mental health.

Francis of Assisi preached and practiced absolute identification with nature, but even his immediate followers soon abandoned his romantic and unworldly attitude. They probably realized that man has never been purely a worshiper of nature or a passive witness of his surroundings and natural events. Human life was naturally close to nature during the Stone Age, but Paleolithic hunters and Neolithic farmers altered their environment. By controlling and using fire, domesticating animals and plants, clearing forests and cultivating crops, they began the process which eventually humanized a large percentage of the earth. Every form of civilization, each in its own way, has since contributed to the shaping of the earth's surface and thus altered

18. Quoted in Paul Fleischman, "Conservation: The Biological Fallacy," *Landscape*, 18 (1969), 26.
19. Fleischman, op. cit.

the composition of the atmosphere and the waters. Even persons who thought they were returning to the ways of nature usually transformed their environment more than they knew. "Sometimes as I drift idly along Walden Pond, I cease to live and I begin to be," Thoreau wrote in his *Journal.* But he used a canoe to drift on the pond and he cleared an area along its shore to grow beans and construct his cabin.

Thus, human life inevitably implies changes in nature. Indeed, man shapes his humanness in the very process of interacting constructively with the world around him and molding nature to make it better suited to his needs, wishes, and aspirations. Stonehenge, Angkor Wat, the Parthenon, the Buddhist temples, and the countless other places of worship created by man before the Judeo-Christian era represent forms of human intervention which exacted as large a toll from nature as did the construction of the Judeo-Christian shrines or the immense American bridges and industrial plants.

Christianity acknowledged early that human beings differ in their spiritual needs and aspirations; each of its important saints symbolizes a different approach to the human problem. In the article quoted earlier, Lynn White, Jr., suggests that Saint Francis's example can help mankind to achieve an harmonious equality with the rest of creation, as if animals, plants, and even inanimate objects were really our brothers and sisters. This doctrine is not quite congenial to me, because I like gardening and landscaping and therefore tend to impose my own sense of order upon natural processes.

Benedict of Nursia, who was certainly as good a Christian as Francis of Assisi, can be regarded as a patron saint of those who believe that true conservation means not only protecting nature against human misbehavior but also developing human activities which favor a creative, harmonious relationship between man and nature.

When Saint Benedict established his monastery on Monte Cassino during the sixth century, his primary concern was that he and his followers should devote their lives to divine worship. However, though he was an aristocrat, he knew the dangers of physical idleness, and he made it a rule that all monks should work with their hands in the fields and in shops. As a result, the Benedictine monks achieved an intimate relationship with the world around them. One of the still dominant aspects of the Benedictine rule is that to labor is to pray. Saint Benedict had not intended his monks to become scholars. But in the course of time a great tradition of learning and of artistic skills progressively developed in the Benedictine abbeys, along with the continuation of some physical work.

Lynn White, Jr., the very historian who has advocated that ecologists take Saint Francis as their patron saint, has also emphasized the social importance of the fact that "the Benedictine monk was the first scholar to get dirt under his fingernails."[20] For the first time in the history of human institutions, the Benedictine abbey created a way of life in which practical and theoretical skills could be embodied in the same person. This new atmosphere proved of enormous importance for the development of European technology and science. The Benedictine abbeys did not immediately launch into scientific investigations, but by encouraging the combination of physical and intellectual work they destroyed the old artificial barrier between the empirical and the speculative, the manual and the liberal arts. This created an atmosphere favorable for the de-

20. Lynn White, Jr., *Machina ex Deo* (Cambridge, Mass.: M.I.T. Press, 1968), 65.

velopment of knowledge based on experimentation.

The first chapter of Genesis speaks of man's dominion over nature. The Benedictine rule in contrast seems inspired rather from the second chapter, in which the Good Lord placed man in the Garden of Eden not as a master but rather in a spirit of stewardship. Throughout the history of the Benedictine order, its monks have actively intervened in nature—as farmers, builders, and scholars. They have brought about profound transformations of soil, water, fauna, and flora, but in such a wise manner that their management of nature has proved compatible in most cases with the maintenance of environmental quality. To this extent, Saint Benedict is much more relevant than Saint Francis to human life in the modern world, and to the human condition in general.

The Benedictine rule was so successful during the early Middle Ages that its monasteries burgeoned over Europe, and their numbers reached many thousands. They differed somewhat in their interpretation of the rule, but all were organized along similar religious and social patterns. All the Benedictine monks and nuns accepted the cloistered life and regarded manual labor not as a regrettable necessity but as an essential part of spiritual discipline. They practiced a democratic administrative system of home rule and tried to achieve a living relationship with the physical world around them. The monastic rule was so broadly human that it permitted different attitudes toward nature and man. For example, while the original Benedictines generally settled on the hills, the monks of the Cistercian branch preferred the valleys. This topographical variation in the location of the monasteries proved to be of great economic and technological significance because it broadened the influence of the Benedictines in the development of Europe.

The Cistercians played a social role of particular importance precisely in this regard, because they established their monasteries in wooded river valleys and marshy lands which were infested with malaria and therefore ill suited to human occupation. With their lay helpers, they cleared the forests and drained the swamps, thus creating, out of the malarious wilderness, farmlands that became healthy and prosperous. They achieved such great fame in the control of malaria by eliminating the swamps that they were entrusted with the task of draining the Roman Campagna.

Cistercian life was of course not motivated by the desire to create agricultural lands. A mystic attitude toward nature certainly played a role in their selection of secluded places for the worship of God. Saint Bernard was sensitive to the poetic quality of the site when he chose to establish his Cistercian monastery in Clairvaux:

> *That spot has much charm, it greatly soothes weary minds, relieves anxieties and cares, helps souls who seek the Lord greatly to devotion, and recalls to them the thought of the heavenly sweetness to which they aspire. The smiling countenance of the earth is painted with varying colours, the blooming verdure of spring satisfies the eyes, and its sweet odour salutes the nostrils. . . . While I am charmed without by the sweet influence of the beauty of the country, I have not less delight within in reflecting on the mysteries which are hidden beneath it.*[21]

Saint Bernard believed that it was the duty of the monks to work as partners of God in improving his creation or at least in giving it a more human expression. Implicit in his writings is the thought that labor is like a prayer which helps in re-creating paradise out of chaotic wilderness.[22]

21. Quoted in Glacken, op. cit., 214.
22. Clarence Glacken, op. cit., 213.

While the primary commitment of the monks was to divine worship, they devoted much effort and inventiveness to practical problems:

> *Cistercian monks were so devoted to the Virgin that everyone of their hundreds of monasteries was dedicated to her; yet these White Benedictines seem often to have led the way in the use of power. Some of their abbeys had four or five water wheels, each powering a different workshop.*[23]

All types of Benedictine monasteries, in fact, were involved in technological activities. The monks developed windmills and especially watermills as sources of power on their holdings. This power was used for the conversion of their agricultural products into manufactured goods—leather, fabrics, paper, and even liqueurs such as Benedictine and Chartreuse, which achieved world-wide fame. Thus these medieval monasteries prepared the ground for the technological era in Europe.

When practiced in the true spirit of the Benedictine rule, monastic life helped the monks to establish close contact with the natural world through the daily and seasonal rituals and works which were coordinated with cosmic rhythms. The Benedictine rule also inspired a type of communal organization which was both democratic and hierarchic, because each monk or nun had rights in the monastic organization but also had to accept a certain place in the social order. This complex social structure found its expression in an architectural style beautifully adapted to the rituals of monastic life and to the local landscape. Benedictine architecture, in its several variant forms, thus achieved a functional beauty which made it a major artistic achievement of Western civilization.[24]

23. White, *Machina ex Deo,* 67.
24. Wolfgang Braunfels, "Institutions and Their Corresponding Ideals," in *The*

Many human interventions into natural systems have been destructive. Technological man in particular uses landscapes and water, mountains and estuaries, and all types of natural resources for selfish and short-range economic benefits. But his behavior in this regard is not much worse than that of the people whose activities caused erosion in West Pakistan, in the Mediterranean basin, in China, or in Mexico. The solution to the environmental crisis will not be found in a retreat from the Judeo-Christian tradition or from technological civilization. Rather it will require a new definition of progress, based on better knowledge of nature and on a willingness to change our ways of life accordingly. We must learn to recognize the limitations and potentialities of each particular area of the earth, so that we can manipulate it creatively, thereby enhancing present and future human life.

Conservation, according to Leopold, teaches what a land can be, what it should be, what it *ought* to be. Although this aphorism has much appeal, it is misleading because it implies a questionable philosophy of ecological determinism and of man's relation to nature. It assumes that some invisible hand is guiding biological processes to the one perfect state of ecological harmony among the different components of a particular environment, whereas experience shows that different satisfactory ecosystems can be created out of the same set of environmental conditions. The aphorism seems to suggest, moreover, that man should not interfere with the natural course of ecological events, a view which does not square with the existence all over the world of successful parks, gardens, agricultural fields, and managed forests.

Fitness of Man's Environment (Washington, D.C.: Smithsonian Institution Press, 1968).

Francis of Assisi's loving and contemplative reverence in the face of nature survives today in the awareness of man's kinship to all other living things and in the conservation movement. But reverence is not enough, because man has never been a passive witness of nature. He changes the environment by his very presence and his only options in his dealings with the earth are to be destructive or constructive. To be creative, man must relate to nature with his senses as much as with his common sense, with his heart as much as with knowledge. He must read the book of external nature and the book of his own nature, to discern the common patterns and harmonies.

Repeatedly in the past and under a great variety of religious traditions and social systems, man has created from wilderness new environments which have proven ecologically viable and culturally desirable. Because of my own cultural tradition, I have chosen to illustrate this creativeness by the Benedictine way of life—its wisdom in managing the land, in fitting architecture to worship and landscape, in adapting rituals and work to the cosmic rhythms. An Australian aborigine, a Navajo Indian, a Buddhist, or a Moslem would have selected other examples, taken from their respective traditions, but the fundamental theme is universal because it deals with man's unique place in the cosmos. Human life implies choices as to the best way to govern natural systems and to create new environments out of wilderness. Reverence for nature is compatible with willingness to accept responsibility for a creative stewardship of the earth.

The Religious Background of the Present Environmental Crisis

ARNOLD TOYNBEE

For about 200 years by now, the progress of the Industrial Revolution has been accelerating. It has spread from Britain round the World. Today the gross national product of Japan, for instance, is second only to that of the United States. At the same time, the Industrial Revolution has been increasing in potency. In the nineteenth century, its continual triumphs were applauded by its beneficiaries—though not by its more numerous victims. Within the last quarter of a century, however, everyone, including the beneficiaries, has rather suddenly become aware of the large and sinister entries on the debit side of the account.

The manufacture, and the use for genocide, of two atomic bombs in 1945 made it impossible for us to shut our eyes any longer to the truth that technology is a morally neutral instrument for enhancing human power, and that, like the jinn who was the slave of Aladdin's lamp, it can be put to work either for good or for evil, according to the will of its human master. We then realized that, even if we were to achieve the difficult political feat of making it impossible for atomic energy ever again to

SOURCE: *International Journal of Environmental Studies,* 3 (1972), 141–146. Reprinted by permission of the author and the *Journal.*

be used in warfare, its use for peaceful purposes will confront us with the problem of disposing innocuously of poisonous atomic waste—a by-product of industrial production that would be far more noxious than coal-smog or even than petrol-fumes.

Within the last 2 or 3 years we have awoken to the truth that atomic poisoning is merely one arresting example of a phenomenon that is older and more general. Since the outbreak of the Industrial Revolution, man has been progressively polluting his environment, and this in two ways. He has been using up natural resources, such as metals and coal and mineral oil, that are irreplaceable, and, by employing these resources for industrial production solely with an eye to immediate profit, he has been spoiling for posterity those parts of the natural environment that he has not already consumed.

MAN'S IMPROVIDENCE

What is the explanation of the improvidence that has now alarmed us and put us to shame? The superficial explanation is that man, like every other living being, is greedy. The capacity and the impulse to try to exploit the rest of the Universe is another name for life itself. Man's greed differs from the greed of other living beings, not in the strength of the impulse, but in the degree of the capacity. Our ancestors became human in the act of inventing tools to do the job, and, within the last two centuries, we have discovered how to increase the potency of our tools enormously. We have achieved this by harnessing one after another of the physical forces of inanimate nature, which are more potent than human or even animal muscle-power. Till then, we had harnessed wind for propelling the sails of ships and windmills, and had harnessed water, as well as wind, for grinding corn. Since then, we have harnessed a host of inanimate forces, from water-power to atomic energy, for making a multitude of things besides the miller's flour that is "the staff of life." Here, manifestly, we have the immediate cause of the genocide at Hiroshima and Nagasaki and of the world-wide pollution that, by now, has become a second cause for anxiety over the possibility that the technological triumph of harnessing atomic energy may have catastrophic results for human life.

All this is obvious, but it is equally obvious that it is only the latest chapter of a long and unfinished story. We must push our inquiry farther back and we must also look ahead. The Industrial Revolution erupted suddenly, but, like the explosion of the two atomic bombs in 1945, which has been the Industrial Revolution's climax so far, it was the result of deliberately planned preparations. A hundred years earlier, the founding fathers of the Royal Society had set, for themselves and for their successors, the objective of promoting the increase of scientific knowledge, not only for its own sake, but also for the systematic application of it to technology. The Industrial Revolution was the fruit of a preceding century of sustained endeavours along these lines.

What was it that moved the founders of the Royal Society to seek to give this new direction to thought and action? Their motive was their moral recoil from their experience of human behaviour in their own lifetime. The condition of England in the middle decades of the seventeenth century was like the condition of Northern Ireland today. Religious schism, hotted up by fervid theological controversy, had boiled over into civil war. The founders of the Royal Society had been horrified neutrals. They had not only been unwilling to take part, themselves, in the verbal and military hostilities; they were concerned to direct the energies of their countrymen, and of the rest of mankind, into new channels in which their activity would be pacific and beneficent. In science they saw a field of intellectual inquiry which would not, like theology, arouse animosity without being able to arrive at any agreed conclusions. They found a field of this preferable kind in the factual study of nature. In scientific inquiry, people could disagree amicably about the facts till they had settled the points at issue by observation or experiment; and then this verified scientific knowledge could be applied systematically to technology. The founding fathers overlooked the snag that scientific technology could be used for military as well as for peaceful purposes, and there was nothing in their experience to forewarn them that mankind's natural environment might be polluted, and that mankind's own survival might be put in jeopardy, even by "atoms for peace."

MONOTHEISTIC RELIGIONS AND NATURE

The founders of the Royal Society were reacting against a perversion of religion, but they were not themselves un-religious, and, still less, anti-religious. Their first secretary and historian, Sprat, was an Anglican clergyman who became a bishop. In any case, it is difficult to disengage oneself from deeply ingrained habits of thought and feeling, even when that is one's aim. The founders of the Royal Society did want to break with traditional Christian intolerance and animosity, and in this they were successful. Thanks to them and to kindred spirits on the Continent, the Wars of Religion were stopped and toleration was established, before the close of the seventeenth century, throughout Europe. Present-day Northern Ireland is a miniature "living museum" of Europe's pre-eighteenth century condition. But, in combatting intolerance and violence, the pioneers of the "Enlightenment" were not challenging the Christian doctrine about the relations between God, man, and nature.

This doctrine is enunciated in one sentence within one verse in the Bible. "Be fruitful and multiply and replenish the Earth and subdue it" (Gen. i, 28). Here was Biblical sanction for the Royal Society's agenda. According to the Bible, God had created the World; the World was his to do what he liked with it; he had chosen to licence Adam and Eve to do what *they* liked with it; and their licence was not cancelled by the Fall. The tenant who had been parked in the Garden, rent-free, was now rack-rented. "In the sweat of thy face shalt thou eat bread" (Gen. iii, 19). But, as an offset, the disgraced human tenant was expelled from the Garden and was let loose on the wide world, and he was not prohibited from easing the payment of his punitive rent to God by harnessing natural forces that could relieve him of having to sweat by doing his work for him. Genesis i, 28, gave the licence; Genesis iii, 19, provided the incentive. In 1661, this read like a blessing on the wealth of Abraham in children and livestock; in 1971, it reads like a licence for the population-explosion, and like both a licence and an incentive for mechanization and pollution.

Read in this alarming present-day sense, these Biblical texts impel the reader to question the truth and the validity of the doctrine that they proclaim. Has the Universe really been created by a unique God who is super-human in power but is human-like in the arbitrariness of his use of his power? Supposing that he exists, has he really handed over to one of his creatures, man, all the rest of his creation? And has nature no rights against this autocratic creator and against man, God's aggressive licensee?

If one has been brought up as a Christian, Jew, or Muslim,

one has been conditioned to take monotheism, and the mundane implications of monotheism, for granted. I myself was brought up in the same sect of Christianity as Bishop Sprat. But I was also educated in pre-Christian Greek and Latin literature; my pre-Christian education has had a deeper and more enduring effect on my *Weltanschauung* than my Christian upbringing; and, even if I had continued to be more of a Christian than a Hellene, my Hellenic education would at least have made me aware that the religion of my pre-Christian predecessors at the western end of the Old World had been a different kind of religion from monotheism.

PRE-MONOTHEISTIC ATTITUDES

When our pre-human ancestors became human through becoming conscious, they found themselves in an environment that they had not made or chosen for themselves, and they became aware that they were at this natural environment's mercy. Of course they promptly started to change it into something that was more to their liking. Technology was initiated by the first of our ancestors who chipped a stone to turn it into a more serviceable tool than it had been in its pristine natural shape; and man's technology is not the oldest on Earth. The beaver anticipated man in constructing barrages, and the termite in erecting Towers of Babel. However, man, being conscious of the Universe and of his own dealings with it, stood in awe of nature's power, even when he had begun to tamper with nature in order to ease his own labour and to satisfy his own greed.

For pre-monotheistic man, nature was not just a treasure-trove of "natural resources." Nature was, for him, a goddess, "Mother Earth," and the vegetation that sprang from the Earth, the animals that roamed, like man himself, over the Earth's surface, and the minerals hiding in the Earth's bowels, all partook of nature's divinity. For primitive man, the whole of his environment was divine, and his sense of nature's divinity outlasted his technological feats of cultivating plants and domesticating animals. In a sense, man has been the creator of his cultivated plants and his domesticated animals; for he has transformed their nature to serve his own needs. Yet, for pre-monotheistic man, wheat and rice were not just "cereals"; they were Ceres herself, the goddess who had allowed man to cultivate these life-giving plants and had taught him the art.

In the pre-Christian Greek World, the deification of nature outlasted the rise of philosophy. I have read somewhere (I have not verified this) that, in Aristotle's scientific survey of the Earth's flora and fauna, a conspicuous omission is the butterfly; Aristotle has not described this insect, and the reason—so it has been suggested—is that unsophisticated pre-Christian Greeks believed that butterflies were the souls of dead human beings. It is most improbable that Aristotle himself believed this, but it is a plausible guess that he forebore to describe butterflies because he would have described them with a scientific objectivity that, for his unsophisticated Greek contemporaries, would have been shockingly irreverent. If so, Aristotle was behaving like a present-day post-Christian agnostic who, if male, takes off his hat on entering a Christian church. He does not believe that, inside the church-door, he is in God's presence. His motive for still observing a Christian ritual practice is not superstition; it is considerateness towards his still croyant contemporaries.

In popular pre-Christian Greek religion, divinity was inherent in all natural phenomena, including those that man had tamed and domesticated. Divinity was present in springs and rivers and the sea; in trees, both the wild oak and the cultivated olive-tree; in corn and vines; in mountains; in earthquakes and lightning and thunder. The god-head was diffused throughout the phenomena. It was plural, not singular; a pantheon, not a unique almighty super-human person. When the Graeco-Roman World was converted to Christianity, the divinity was drained out of nature and was concentrated in one unique transcendent God. "Pan is dead." "The oracles are dumb." Bronsgrove is no longer a wood that is sacrosanct because it is animated by the god Bron. It is true that, at the level of folk-religion, the pre-monotheistic religion of mankind has lived on under a monotheistic veneer. The local divinities have been replaced by saints; but officially a saint, even Mary "the Mother of God," is not even a minor god, but is merely a human being who has found favour in the unique God's sight by having been obedient to his commands. Christianity, alone among the three Judaic monotheistic religions, dilutes its monotheism by giving God the Father two associates and equals in God the Son and God the Holy Spirit.

It is impossible to become familiar with pre-Christian Greek and Latin literature without also becoming acquainted with Graeco-Roman religion and seeing nature, with pre-Christian eyes, as being animated by divinity. At the western end of the Old World, this nature-worship, which is the original religion of all mankind, has been overlaid by an opaque veneer of Christianity and Islam; but, when a native of the monotheistic portion of the present-day World travels eastward beyond the easternmost limits of Islam, he finds himself in a living pre-monotheistic World, and, if he has had a Greek and Latin education which he has taken seriously, the religion of present-day East Asia will be more familiar to him, and also more congenial to him, than the religion of the West, in which the traveller himself has been brought up. For instance, when I myself visit Japan, I find myself being constantly reminded, by present-day Japanese religious shrines and sites, of Saint Augustine's description of the pre-Christian religion of the Romans.

EASTERN RELIGIONS

My observation of the living religion of Eastern Asia, and my book-knowledge of the extinguished Greek and Roman religion, has made me aware of the startling and disturbing truth that monotheism, as enunciated in the Book of Genesis, has removed the age-old restraint that was once placed on man's greed by his awe. Man's greedy impulse to exploit nature used to be held in check by his pious worship of nature. This primitive inhibition has been removed by the rise and spread of monotheism. Moreover, the monotheistic disrespect for nature has survived the weakening of the belief in monotheism in the ex-monotheistic part of the World, and it has invaded that major portion of the World in which monotheism has never become established.

In this context the modern history and present plight of Japan are particularly significant. Japanese converts to Christianity have been few, though some of them have been eminent; but the Christian attitude to nature, which continues to be the post-Christian attitude, has prevailed in Japan in defiance of the contrary *Weltanschauung* that is implicit in the Japanese people's ancestral religions, Shinto and Buddhism. Since the Meiji Revolution of 1868, and with re-doubled vehemence since the end of the Second World War, the Japanese have been following the modern Western malpractice of exploiting nature, and they have been incurring the penalty. They have been winning wealth by industrialization and have been reaping pollution from it. Both the increase in the gross national product and the increase in pollution have been more sensational in post-war Japan than anywhere else in the World. Japan's present plight illustrates the truth that the evil consequences of monotheism's revolutionary overthrow of the traditional balance between man and nature can work havoc even where monotheism itself has never gained any appreciable foothold.

THE PRESENT ECOLOGICAL CRISIS AND RELIGION

The thesis of the present essay is that some of the major maladies of the present-day world—for instance the recklessly extravagant consumption of nature's irreplaceable treasures, and the pollution of those of them that man has not already devoured—can be traced back in the last analysis to a religious cause, and that this cause is the rise of monotheism. It is now widely recognized that, in order to secure the survival of mankind, we in our generation are going to have to make a revolutionary reversal of the order of priorities that has governed our behaviour since the outbreak of the Industrial Revolution.

For the last 200 years, we have given priority to the maximization of material wealth, regardless of the price in human suffering and in the wrecking of the natural environment from which our wealth has been extracted by the modern device of mechanization. From now on, we shall have to give priority to the re-humanization of human life and to the conservation of what we have left of our natural environment, whatever the cost of this may be in limiting, and probably reducing, the World's gross global product. A religious revolution opened the door for us to pursue our recent lethal course. Does not this historical fact indicate that a religious counter-revolution will be needed for inspiring us and nerving us to retrace our steps before we reach the precipice that yawns close ahead of us along our present Gadarene course?

For people who have been brought up in the monotheist tradition, it is difficult to re-gain the awe of nature that was shattered by the pronouncement in Genesis i, 28. Even for the majority of the present generation that has never been, or has now ceased to be, monotheistic, it has become difficult to recover the conviction that nature, as well as man, has rights, and that, if man violates nature's rights, nature will take her revenge on man. Yet surely she is taking her revenge on us unmistakably in our time. Modern man has finally succeeded in smothering man's natural environment under an artificial man-made environment; but man has no sooner accomplished this than he has found that he has made life intolerable for himself.

We have been taking unlimited liberties with nature because we have been thinking of her, in monotheistic terms, as unsacrosanct "raw material." But, under this test, nature has proved to be indispensable, after all, for mankind's welfare and perhaps even for its existence. We have discovered that, in the last resort, we are still as much at nature's mercy as our pre-human ancestors were. If man de-natures the air and water and soil of this planet, he is not going to be able to survive. Nature is still our mistress; she, not man, has the last word. This truth has been re-impressed on our minds by our current experience. Does not this suggest that we ought to stop taking the monotheistic *Weltanschauung* for granted?

Monotheism is exceptional among mankind's religions and philosophies in its doctrine about what is the right relation between man and nature. The Book of Genesis licences man to subdue nature. Confucianism and Taoism and Shinto, like the pre-Christian Greek cults of the corn-goddess Demeter (Ceres, in Latin) and the wine-god Dionysus, counsel man to respect nature even when he is applying his human science to coax nature into bestowing her bounty on man. The sanctuary at Ise, in Japan, which is the chief holy place of Shinto, is sited at a meeting-point of rice-paddies and virgin forest. The location of the Ise shrine signifies that man should beware of losing his respect for the divinity inherent in the Earth's flora, even when he cultivates it. And in fact, when a Westerner talks with the Japanese about rice-cultivation, he finds that, for them, this is not just an economic activity, though they pursue it with marvellous technological efficiency; rice-cultivation in Japan is still also a religious rite, as agriculture was everywhere at the beginning.

The heart of Confucius's teaching is that the key to righteousness and welfare is the attainment and the maintenance of harmony, and that, if human beings break the due harmony between man and nature, they will fall into discord among themselves. According to pre-Christian Greek legend, the wine-god Dionysus took a terrible revenge on a king who had maltreated him and on pirates who had kidnapped him in blind ignorance of who and what he was. The Greek temper was more violent and vindictive than the Chinese, but the Dionysiac Greek religion and the Confucian Chinese philosophy teach the same lesson.

THE REMEDY

If I am right in my diagnosis of mankind's present-day distress, the remedy lies in reverting from the *Weltanschauung* of monotheism to the *Weltanschauung* of pantheism, which is older and was once universal. The plight in which post-

Industrial-Revolution man has now landed himself is one more demonstration that man is not the master of his environment—not even when supposedly armed with a warrant, issued by a supposedly unique and omnipotent God with a human-like personality, delegating to man plenipotentiary powers. Nature is now demonstrating to us that she does not recognize the validity of this alleged warrant, and she is warning us that, if man insists on trying to execute it, he will commit this outrage on nature at his peril.

If the cogent evidence for divinity were really power, Dionysus and Demeter and Zeus and Poseidon, who are now re-asserting their power, would be more credible gods than Yahweh; for they are demonstrating to present-day man that he cannot pollute soil, air, and water with impunity. However, the founders of the less crude religions and philosophies have perceived that the nature of divinity is not power but love, benevolence, and humanity (the concept conveyed in the Chinese word *jen*). The Buddha, the Bodhisattvas and Christ stand, not for the exercise of power, but for self-abnegation and self-sacrifice; and it is significant that the figure of Christ has dissolved monolithic Jewish monotheism into the Christian Trinity. Confucianism and Shinto stand for a harmonious cooperation between man and nature. Taoism stands for letting nature take her course, undisturbed by impertinent and clumsy human interference. Surely the *Weltanschauung* that follows from these more perceptive and less aggressive religious and philosophical traditions is the one that now offers the most promising hope of salvaging mankind. The injunction to "subdue," which modern man has taken as his directive, is surely immoral, impracticable, and disastrous.

Contributors

James Barr is Professor of Semitic Languages and Literature at Manchester University, England. Among his books are *The Semantics of Biblical Language* and *Comparative Philology and the Text of the Old Testament.*

René Dubos is a professor emeritus at Rockefeller University. He is the author of many scientific works, including, on ecology, *Man Adapting, So Human an Animal,* and *A God Within.*

John Macquarrie is Lady Margaret Professor of Divinity at Oxford University. He is the author of many books, including *An Existential Theology, Twentieth Century Religious Thought,* and *Principles of Christian Theology.*

Lewis W. Moncrief is Associate Professor and Director of the Recreation and Planning Unit and holds a joint appointment in the Department of Park and Recreation Resources and Resource Development at Michigan State University. He is the compiler of *A Bibliography on Leisure.*

Arnold Toynbee is professor emeritus of the University of London. He is the author of the monumental *A Study of History.*

Yi-Fu Tuan is Professor of Geography at the University of Minnesota. He is the author of *The Hydrologic Cycle and the Wisdom of God.*

Lynn White, Jr., is Professor of History at the University of California. He is President of the History of Science Society (1973) and President of the American History Association (1974). His books include *Medieval Technology and Social Change* and *Machina ex Deo.*

Selected Bibliography

Barbour, Ian, ed. *Earth Might Be Fair.* Englewood Cliffs, N.J., 1972

———, ed. *Western Man and Environmental Ethics.* Reading, Mass., 1973.

Bates, Marston. *The Forest and the Sea.* New York, 1960.

Black, John. *Dominion of Man.* Edinburgh, 1970.

Cox, Harvey. *The Secular City.* New York, 1965.

Dorst, Jean. *Before Nature Dies.* Boston, 1970.

Dubos, René. *A God Within.* New York, 1972.

Elder, Frederick. *Crisis in Eden.* Nashville, Tenn., 1970.

Ellul, Jacques. *The Technological Society.* New York, 1964.

Elton, Charles. *The Ecology of Invasions by Animals and Plants.* London, 1958.

Glacken, Clarence. *Traces on the Rhodian Shore.* Berkeley, 1967.

Hamilton, Michael, ed. *This Little Planet.* New York, 1970.

Jacobs, Wilbur R. "Frontiersmen, Fur Traders and Other Varmints, an Ecological Appraisal of the Frontier in American History." *American Historical Association Newsletter,* 8 (November 1970), 5–11.

Krutch, Joseph Wood. *The Great Chain of Life.* Boston, 1957.

———. *The World of Animals.* New York, 1961.

Leopold, Aldo. *A Sand County Almanac.* New York, 1949.

Moule, C. D. F. *Man and Nature in the New Testament.* Philadelphia, 1967.

Mumford, Lewis. *Myth of the Machine.* 2 vols. New York, 1967–70.

Nicholson, E. Max. *The Environmental Revolution.* London, 1970

Santmire, Paul. *Brother Earth.* New York, 1970.

Shepard, Paul and McKinley, Daniel, eds. *The Subversive Science.* Boston, 1969.

Stone, Glenn C., ed. *A New Ethic for a New Earth.* New York, 1971.

Turner, E. S. *All Heaven in a Rage.* London, 1964.

Westermarck, E. A. *Christianity and Morals.* London, 1939.

White, Lynn, Jr. "The Iconography of *Temperantia* and the Virtuousness of Technology." In *Action and Conviction in Early Modern Europe: Essays in Memory of E. H. Harbison,* edited by T. K. Rabb and J. E. Seigel, pp. 197–219. Princeton, 1969.

———. *Machina ex Deo: Essays in the Dynamism of Western Culture.* Cambridge, Mass., 1968.

———. *Medieval Technology and Social Change.* Oxford, 1962.

———. "Natural Science and Naturalistic Art in the Middle Ages." *American Historical Review,* 52 (1947), 421–435.

Wynne-Edwards, V. C. *Animal Dispersion in Relation to Social Behavior.* New York, 1962.

———. "Self-Regulating Systems in Populations of Animals." *Science,* 147 (26 March 1965), 1543–1548.